DUTCH OVEN
AND CAST IRON
COOKING

**Revised & Expanded
Second Edition**

DUTCH OVEN AND CAST IRON COOKING

COOKING

**Revised & Expanded
Second Edition**

Foreword by Colleen Sloan,
author of *Log Cabin Dutch Oven*

FOX CHAPEL
PUBLISHING

Recipe selection, design, and book design © 2017 Fox Chapel Publishing Company, Inc., 903 Square Street, Mount Joy, PA 17552.

Except as noted below, all recipes and photography © 2017 G&R Publishing DBA CQ Products.

The Publisher would like to thank Donna and Colleen Sloan of A Happy Camper (*www.ahappycamper.com*) for sharing their recipes and tips in this book.

The recipes on pages 40 and 50 courtesy of Colleen Sloan and A Happy Camper (*www.ahappycamper.com*).

The text appearing on pages 10–12, 18–25, the sidebar on page 16, and the chart on page 26 courtesy of Colleen Sloan and A Happy Camper (*www.ahappycamper.com*).

Source for About Colleen Sloan (page 12): Carrie A. Moore, "Going Dutch: Utahn Is Expert at Cooking with Cast Iron and Coals," *Deseret News*, July 14, 2004, *www.deseretnews.com/article/595076993/Going-Dutch-Utahn-is-expert-atcooking-with-cast-iron-and-coals.html*.

The Publisher would like to thank Ashley Burnstad, Le Creuset, Lodge Manufacturing Company, Emily Loeffelman, Tracy Melton, Kyle Murphy, Tasneem Rajkotwala, David G. Smith, Ruth Tam, Christie Vanover, and Beth Velatini for kindly sharing their photos (pages noted below).

Ashley Burnstad (*www.ashleyburnstad.com*, *@ashleyburnstadphoto*): 27, 169, and the cover

Le Creuset (*www.lecreuset.com*): 15, 29 (right), and 133

Lodge Manufacturing Company (*lodgemfg.com*): 10, 13, 26, 28 (skillets), and 30

Emily Loeffelman (*www.everythingemilyblog.com*, *@emilyloeffelman*): 19

Tracy Melton (*focuslineart.bigcartel.com*, *@focuslineart*): 3

Kyle Murphy (*knmportraits.com*, *@knmportraits*): 33 and 145

Tasneem Rajkotwala (*www.thoughtsoverchai.net*, *@thoughtsoverchai*): 5, 37, and 43

David G. Smith (*www.panman.com*), photos and captions: 46, 71, 75, 120, 129, 151, 159, and 170

Ruth Tam (*cooktildelicious.com*, *@rushyama*): 59

Christie Vanover (*www.instagram.com/girlscangrill*): 199

Beth Velatini (*www.instagram.com/mybizzykitchen*): 41

ISBN 978-1-56523-911-1

Library of Congress Cataloging-in-Publication Data

Names: Sloan, Colleen, writer of foreword.
  Title: Dutch oven & cast iron cooking / foreword by Colleen Sloan, author of Log Cabin Dutch Oven.
  Other titles: Dutch oven and cast iron cooking
  Description: Revised and expanded. | East Petersburg : Fox Chapel Publishing, 2017. | Includes index.
  Identifiers: LCCN 2016056257 | ISBN 9781565239111
  Subjects: LCSH: Dutch oven cooking. | Dutch ovens. | LCGFT: Cookbooks.
  Classification: LCC TX840.D88 D885 2017 | DDC 641.5/89--dc23

To learn more about the other great books from Fox Chapel Publishing, or to find a retailer near you, call toll-free 800-457-9112 or visit us at *www.FoxChapelPublishing.com*.

We are always looking for talented authors. To submit an idea, please send a brief inquiry to acquisitions@foxchapelpublishing.com.

Printed in Singapore
Second printing

CONTENTS

BREADS 64

SIDE DISHES 146

DESSERTS 172

INDEX 198

FOREWORD

A Brief History of Cast Iron Cookware

The Dutch oven, once called the black pot or cooking cauldron, has been a popular cooking vessel for centuries. In fact, early references to the black pot can be found in the Old Testament. Columbus brought Dutch oven cooking pots with him on his voyage that led to the discovery of the Americas. In 1620, the Pilgrims cooked with them during their crossing to America, hanging the pots from ship beams and building fires underneath them in sand pits. The Dutch oven is now returning to popularity because of the tasty food it produces and because of the material from which it is made: cast iron.

Cast iron was the material of choice for early cookware because of its ability to withstand high heat, frequent use and some rough handling. Until the start of the eighteenth century, iron was cast in baked loam or clay soil molds. This gave the finished product a rough surface, and the mold generally broke during removal. These early pieces were also very thick walled and heavy. The most advanced foundries of the time were located in or near Holland, and their high-quality cast iron products, including Dutch ovens, were imported to Great Britain and elsewhere in Europe. When people from Europe and Great Britain immigrated to America, they brought the cast iron trade with them.

In 1704, Abraham Darby, an English Quaker, traveled to Holland to inspect the cast iron foundries. As a result, he discovered that wet sand molds could be used to make lighter, thinner cast iron products at a much faster rate than with other methods. In 1708, Darby received a patent for his casting process and began manufacturing large quantities of cast iron products in a furnace at Coalbrookdale. By the mid-eighteenth century, Darby's cast iron pots were being shipped to America.

This image from the mid- to late-1900s shows a Lodge Manufacturing Company employee creating the molds for Lodge's cast iron products.

The first American casting was made in Massachusetts circa 1642, and afterward, small foundries began to appear in most of the colonies. Pots from this time period can often be identified by a round protrusion of extra iron, known as a sprue, formed on the pot where the iron entered the mold. Generally, the sprue is located on the bottom of a pot, so it didn't affect the use of hearth pots, which were suspended over a fire or nestled in a bed of coals. As cooking ranges were developed, however, it became necessary to produce cookware with flat bottoms for use on a stovetop or in the oven of a coal or wood stove.

Two major foundries producing cast iron cookware during the eighteenth century were Griswold Manufacturing Company in Erie,

Pennsylvania, and Wagner Manufacturing Company in Sidney, Ohio. With the invention of artificial nonstick materials like Teflon®, however, the cookware industry began to change, resulting in the closing of many foundries, including Griswold and Wagner. People wanted pots and pans that were lightweight, pretty and pretreated for nonstick cooking. Cast iron skillets, griddles and Dutch ovens were relegated to the back shelf in favor of the newest and "greatest" cookware available.

Today, cast iron cookware is being rediscovered as something that produces mouthwatering foods and is durable enough to be passed down through generations of cooks. These old standbys are one-time purchases with cooking surfaces that get better with age and regular use. Although the Griswold and Wagner foundries are no longer open, they remain well-known names among cast iron enthusiasts and collectors, and other companies, such as Lodge Manufacturing Company, continue to produce outstanding cast iron cookware today.

Some things have changed about Dutch ovens and other cast iron cookware, but they still make excellent cooking tools. It really thrills me to see so many people attending classes and demonstrations about Dutch ovens and cast iron cookware. Cast iron cookware is a lifetime investment and, if cared for, will be a family heirloom you can keep for generations. Make it your way of cooking today and carry on the old traditions.

Try your favorite recipe by warming your Dutch oven and lightly oiling it. Put your food in, heat the oven to 350 degrees, and wait for the smell—it will tell you when it's done. Like my Grandma said, "Kissin' wears out, but cookin' don't." Cook with love—it's the only ingredient missing.

— Colleen Sloan,
author of *Log Cabin Dutch Oven*

About Colleen Sloan

Colleen Sloan grew up on a farm in Utah, where she learned the basics of Dutch oven and camp cooking from her family. Recognizing that this traditional method of cooking was something worth preserving, Sloan has made an effort to bring Dutch oven and cast iron cooking to as many people as possible.

For nearly two decades, Sloan has been introducing others to the delicious taste of food prepared with cast iron cookware. Driving across the country, she gives demonstrations and teaches classes about Dutch oven and camp cooking techniques. She eventually self-published her first cookbook, which features traditional recipes from her grandmother. The venture was largely successful, and several more cookbooks have followed.

To support her cast iron cooking craze, Sloan has a collection of more than 150 cast iron pieces, and that number is always growing. The set includes such standout pieces as a bean pot predating the Revolutionary War.

Today, cast iron products and cooking methods are climbing back into popularity, capturing the interest of people across the country. Sloan is incredibly excited to see this rising interest in the cooking methods she has been using her entire life.

The molten cast iron was poured by hand into sand molds.

The cookware shown here is ready to be distributed to customers.

CAST IRON:
BACK TO THE BASICS

The rediscovery of cast iron cookware begins with learning about cast iron and how to care for it. If you're a new cast iron enthusiast, start here to learn everything you need to know about different cast iron products, how to care for them and how to cook with them. When you've got the basics down, dive into the recipes for some delicious meals that are sure to go on your favorites list. You'll find everything from quick and easy recipes that come together in minutes to hearty, from-scratch dishes. And be sure to keep an eye out for the handy sidebars and vintage spotlights that feature some great info about cast iron cookware.

Cast iron cookware is available bare and covered with an enamel coating. While the recipes in this book focus on the use of bare cast iron cookware, you might find you are attracted to the look of enamelware. See page 29 for some helpful information about the difference between bare and enamel cast iron.

Characteristics of Cast Iron Cookware

It's versatile. Made from a single piece of metal, it can go directly from stovetop to oven and be used with campfires and grills. It will handle any style of cooking that you need—you can sauté, roast, bake and more. You can brown food in a skillet and then transfer it directly into a hot oven to finish cooking. That's one-pot cooking at its best!

It's heavy. This means your cast iron pots and pans will maintain an even cooking temperature once heated. This also means your cast iron cookware is durable, and it only gets better with age. A well-maintained cast iron piece can last for generations! Because it is heavy, look for sturdy handles on both sides to make handling easier, and use both hands to lift and move pans.

It can handle high temperatures. You're going to get great results with cast iron cookware. Food will brown nicely and crusts will be crisp. The pots retain heat, so you can serve meals right out of your cookware without any concern that it will go cold. Do remember to use good pot holders and trivets, though!

It's inexpensive, green cooking. It's not very difficult to manufacture cast iron cookware, so compared to other top-of-the line pots and pans, it's relatively inexpensive. If the price tag is still making you hesitate, keep in mind that if cared for, your cookware will last for years—and probably beyond—and won't have to be replaced any time soon. If you don't want to buy new, shop at second-hand stores or estate sales for used cookware.

It's natural, nonstick cooking. Unlike other nonstick cookware, there are no artificial chemical coatings to be concerned about with cast iron. And if you keep your cast iron pots and pans well seasoned, you will have a natural, nonstick surface—all of the benefits of nonstick cooking without any synthetic materials, just the natural oils you use to season the cookware.

It can add an important nutrient to your food. When you cook with cast iron, a bit of iron leaches from the pan into the food being prepared, bumping up the iron content for your body to absorb. So just by cooking your food, you are making sure your body is well nourished—no extra vegetables or vitamins required! (Acidic foods, like tomato sauces, pull out more iron from the pans, so limit the cooking time of these foods to 30 minutes or less to avoid any metallic taste.)

How Did the Dutch Oven Get Its Name?

Dutch ovens and other cast iron cookware were distributed throughout America by salesmen with wagons. When a salesman or trader was seen coming with his pots clanging on the side hangers of his wagon, people would say, "Here comes the Dutchman with his ovens."

Prepping & Caring for Cast Iron

Seasoning

Seasoning is the process of preparing the cast iron cookware for use. There are two objectives to this process:

1. Coat the cookware to prevent rust
2. Create a natural, permanent, nonstick cooking surface

Seasoning is an easy, but very important, first step when using cast iron cookware. Unlike synthetically coated cookware, cast iron items can be seasoned and their cooking surfaces restored. When you season a cast iron utensil, you

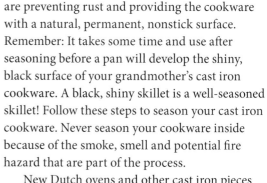

are preventing rust and providing the cookware with a natural, permanent, nonstick surface. Remember: It takes some time and use after seasoning before a pan will develop the shiny, black surface of your grandmother's cast iron cookware. A black, shiny skillet is a well-seasoned skillet! Follow these steps to season your cast iron cookware. Never season your cookware inside because of the smoke, smell and potential fire hazard that are part of the process.

New Dutch ovens and other cast iron pieces have a protective wax coating to prevent rust during shipping. If you have a new cast iron piece, remove any paper labels and place it on heat on a barbecue grill to burn off the protective wax coating.

Lightly grease your cookware, inside and out. Suggested oils for this process include vegetable oil, solid Crisco, bacon grease or lard because they offer a low burning point.

Place your cookware in your barbeque grill or outdoor cook stove. You do not want the oil to pool anywhere in your cookware during the seasoning process, so be sure to turn it bottom side up. If you are seasoning a Dutch oven, put the lid on top of the legs. Heat the cookware on medium heat until it turns black and the oil is burned into the surface. You will want the heat around 500°F–550°F to burn the oil in. If you are using an outdoor cook stove, put about 25–30 briquettes into the stove to reach the proper temperature. You will notice that sometime during this process, smoke will come out of your barbecue grill for about 20 minutes or so. This is normal. Remember, you are burning oil into the pan, creating the nice black look that you want. After one hour, turn off your grill and let the cookware cool by itself. Your cookware will be EXTREMELY hot, so cooling will take some

time. It is helpful to let the cookware sit overnight. Then, it will be cool in the morning.

After your cookware has cooled, check your progress. Your cookware should be a nice black color. If you see what look like freckles on the surface, part of the protective wax coating was not removed before seasoning. To address this, scrub those areas to remove the wax, and then repeat the seasoning process.

If the cookware is not as black as you'd like, repeat the process using a slightly higher heat setting on your grill. Remember, you want your cookware to be black, not brown. A brown color means you need to season at a higher temperature.

Acidic foods, such as tomato sauce, might remove some seasoning. Lightly oil your cookware after preparing acidic foods and place it upside down in your grill for 30 minutes to reseason it.

Cleaning

Pans may be cleaned without water by scrubbing them with coarse salt or a plastic scraper and then simply wiping them with a clean rag or paper towel. They may also be washed with very hot water and a stiff nylon brush or scrubber, rinsed and wiped dry. It's best to avoid dish soap (it strips off the seasoning and can seep into the metal), but if you feel it's necessary to get your pan clean, use it sparingly and then refresh the seasoning.

Natural apple cider vinegar is also an excellent cleaning tool for cast iron. Mix 4 parts water and 1 part vinegar together and put the mixture in a spray bottle. While your cookware is still warm, spray it with the water/vinegar mixture and cover it with the lid for a few minutes. You will notice that any food left in the pan will become soft. Just use coarse salt or a plastic scraper to scrub off the food residue. Then wipe with a clean rag or paper towel. Repeat as necessary.

Drying

Wipe cookware with paper towels or old towels (cast iron can leave black stains). Then, set it on a burner over low heat to remove remaining moisture and prevent rust. Periodically, lightly coat the inside of the warm pan with oil or shortening and return to low heat for 1 to 2 minutes to refresh seasoning. This is only recommended if you intend to use your pan again within a short period of time. Otherwise, do not oil your pan, as the oil can become rancid if left for a long time between uses. Let the pan cool completely before storing. Remember, cast iron cookware can get hot fast! Use a hot pad!

Storing

After all the moisture has been removed from your cookware and it has cooled down, put a paper towel over the top so half hangs inside and half hangs outside the cookware. Then, put the lid on. If you have a storage bag, place the cookware in the bag. Store it in a dry location. Remember not to reseason your cookware before storage unless you intend to use it again immediately. Otherwise, the oil could go rancid before your next use.

Removing rust

If you have inherited an old cast iron piece or stored one that still had some moisture in it, you might encounter rust. If the rust is just beginning to appear, scrub the piece with a scouring pad, sandpaper, steel wool or a rust eraser (available at your local hardware store) and rinse well. Once the rust has been removed, make sure you dry your cookware over a heat source to remove all the moisture. Do not let your cast iron cookware air-dry, as this can promote rust. Then, reseason your cookware.

Profile rust is rust seen and felt on the cookware. To remove this type of rust, use a very fine grade of steel wool or an abrasive soap pad to scrub the affected area. When the piece is scrubbed down to the raw cast iron, it should be reseasoned immediately. If you have put any water on the cookware, you should dry it over heat before reseasoning.

Rust covering the majority of the cast iron is considered severe. You might encounter this on an older piece that has been neglected. You have two options to refurbish this cookware.

First, purchase a metal brush that will fit on a hand drill. Attach the brush to the drill and use it to scrub away the rust. Then, season the pan immediately.

Second, you can soak the cookware in vinegar and water to remove the rust. Place the cookware in a large container and surround it with hay. Fill the container with enough water to cover the pan, adding 2 cups of cider vinegar for every gallon of water. Let the pan soak for about an hour. Then, check to see if the rust has been removed. If not, scrub the pan a little and let it soak for an additional hour. Repeat until all the rust has been removed—this may take 12 to 24 hours if your pan is extremely rusty. Then, scrub it with a scouring pad and rinse and season the pan.

Removing rancid oil

Without frequent use, the oil used for seasoning cast iron can become rancid and affect the taste of your food. To prevent this, do not reseason your pan before storage unless you know you will use it again shortly. If you find your oil has become rancid, you can remove it using the following process.

Put your cookware on a heat source and add 1 cup of vinegar and enough water to fill the pan. Boil the water and vinegar for about 30 minutes. As you boil the water and vinegar, you will see the oil start to pull out of the sides of the cookware. When this occurs, your pan is ready for use. Pour out the water and return the pan to the heat source to dry if you don't plan to use it immediately. If you wish to begin cooking, spray the pan with some oil and you're ready to start!

Caring for Cast Iron

- Don't put cold water into a hot pan (or hot water into a cold one)—it can crack.
- Never leave cast iron soaking in water— it may rust.
- Don't wash cast iron cookware in the dishwasher unless you need to strip the pan to prepare it for the seasoning process.
- Cast iron holds heat, so use thick pot holders when handling pots and pans.
- Enamel-coated cast iron is not designed for outdoor cooking and requires some special care.

Types of Cast Iron Cookware

Dutch oven: A deep, thick-walled cooking pot with a tight-fitting lid.

Camp-style Dutch oven: Used primarily for cooking with a campfire.

Features: 3 short legs, flat lid with a vertical lip (to hold hot coals), sturdy cast iron handle on lid, strong wire handle attached at the sides (to lift or hang pot).

Kitchen-style Dutch oven: Used for cooking on a stovetop, in an oven, or on a grate or propane burner.

Features: Flat bottom, domed or rounded lid (it won't hold coals), sturdy handle on lid and each side, optional wire handle (to lift or hang pot).

Buying tips: Though you can purchase many different sizes, a 10" and/or 12" Dutch oven (3" to 4" deep) will be most useful for general cooking. A 10" Dutch oven can be stacked on top of a larger one during cooking to share coals and space.

COOKING WITH VARIOUS DUTCH OVEN SIZES		
Diameter	**Volume**	**Uses**
5"	1 pint	Melt butter, make basting sauce, make individual desserts
6"	1 quart	Prepare small portions of recipes or sauces
8"	2 quarts	Prepare sauces, toppings or vegetables, warm leftovers
10"	4 quarts	Prepare a complete meal for two; prepare soups, cornbread, main dishes or side dishes
10"	5 quarts	Prepare main or side dishes
12"	6 quarts	Prepare main or side dishes
12"	8 quarts	Prepare whole chicken or roast, bread, or standing rib roast; prepare main or side dishes
14"	8 quarts	Prepare meals for larger groups, such as a roast with vegetables, large stews or cobblers
14"	10 quarts	Roast a small turkey or ham, bake a large batch of bread, prepare large meals or side dishes
16"	12 quarts	Use to double any recipes calling for a 12" oven, prepare large meals or side dishes

To build a good nonstick patina on new cookware, cook foods with a high fat content the first few times you use it. For example, cooking bacon or sausage or frying chicken or donuts helps oil seep into the pores of cast iron.

Skillet: A heavy frying pan (1" to 3" deep), usually round, with or without a lid. Used for cooking on a stovetop, in an oven, or on a grate or propane burner.

Buying tips: Though skillets come in different diameters, consider buying a small skillet (5" to 8") for sautéing vegetables and a larger skillet (10" to 12") with a lid for all-purpose cooking. When purchasing larger skillets, look for an assist handle opposite the long handle to make lifting easier.

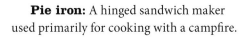

Pie iron: A hinged sandwich maker used primarily for cooking with a campfire.

Buying tips: Make sure the two halves of your pie iron can be separated for easy cleaning and seasoning. Pie irons come in circular and square shapes. Try purchasing one of each for a variety of recipes. If you often camp in large groups, you might want to consider a larger pie iron that can handle two pies or sandwiches at once.

The Enamel Enigma

Cast iron cookware without any sort of coating is known as bare cast iron, while cast iron that has then been coated with a layer of porcelain is known as enamel cast iron. If you are looking to add a cast iron piece to your kitchen collection, it's important to know the pros and cons of each.

Bare Cast Iron

Pros:

- Durable
- Able to withstand high heat
- Even heating surface
- Nonstick surface
- Affordable
- Infuses food with a bit of iron

Cons:

- Requires regular seasoning and care to prevent rust
- Can retain strong food flavors
- Should not be used to prepare acidic foods/sauces

Enamel Cast Iron

Pros:

- Even heating surface
- No seasoning required
- Protective coating eliminates the chance of rust
- Won't retain food flavors
- Can be used to prepare acidic foods/sauces
- Available in lots of colors

Cons:

- Enamel is not a nonstick surface
- High heat can damage or discolor the coating
- More expensive than bare cast iron

What does this mean for you? Give both bare and enamel cast iron a shot and see which you prefer. It's likely you'll enjoy using the bare cast iron for certain types of recipes and the enamel cast iron for others.

Note: For the recipes in this book, we recommend bare cast iron cookware.

Griddle: A large flat grilling surface, usually oblong or round, with a short vertical lip around the edges. Used for cooking on a stovetop (or occasionally, in an oven). Large griddles may straddle two burners if there is space between the griddle and the enameled stovetop, but limit the cooking time to avoid damage to the stovetop. Also used for cooking on a grate or propane burner (depending upon size).

Buying tips: Choose a size and shape that will hold the quantity of food you wish to cook at one time and one that fits on your cooking equipment. Look for a handle at both ends for easy lifting. Consider a reversible griddle with ridges on one side if you grill meat often (ridges hold meat above the heat and grease).

Cast iron accessories

If you find you're using your cast iron cookware often, especially outdoors, you might appreciate these cast iron additions to help make your cooking safe and easy.

Charcoal chimney starter: Tool to light charcoal briquettes more quickly.

Lid lifter: Tool to remove a Dutch oven lid without dumping hot coals or ashes into the pot.

Long tongs: Tool to move hot coals safely.

Heavy-duty pot holders/leather gloves: To protect hands when handling hot cookware.

Cooking Methods

Oven & Stovetop

Use the stovetop and/or oven of a standard gas or electric range and set temperatures as indicated in recipes. Cookware to use: skillets, griddles and kitchen-style Dutch ovens. If using a glass cooktop, follow the manufacturer's directions and be sure the bottoms of the pans are perfectly flat and smooth. Lift the cookware to move it; do not slide or drop it. To use a camp-style Dutch oven in a standard kitchen oven, straddle its three legs over the rungs of the oven rack. Pull out rack and carefully lift the pot to move it.

Grill & Campfire

On a campfire, burn wood or charcoal briquettes to produce heat (coals), or use a gas grill with a grate or burner. Control the cooking temperature by the number and placement of hot coals, the distance of a grate above the heat and the placement of the cookware. Add fresh hot coals as needed to maintain the cooking temperature until the food is done. Rotate the cookware every 10 to 15 minutes to avoid uneven cooking or burn spots. Cooking on a grate usually requires a little extra time.

Skillets: Place a skillet on a grate directly over hot coals or gas grill heat. For a lower temperature, slide the pan to one side, away from the heat (indirect heat). Use skillets with or without a lid.

Griddles: Place a griddle on a grate directly over hot coals or gas grill heat; move it to the side to reduce cooking temperatures (indirect heat). For griddles to perform well outside, they need even heat.

Pie irons: Place a pie iron directly on hot coals or on a grate. For a lower temperature, move it to the side or hold it above coals. Flip the iron for even cooking.

Dutch ovens: Place a Dutch oven directly on hot coals or on a grate, or hang it over a fire. To rotate, lift the pot and turn it ¼ to ⅓ turn in one direction before setting it back on the heat. (Setting the legs back into vacated spaces between coals makes this easy.) Turn the lid ¼ to ⅓ turn in the opposite direction.

The number of coals you use and the way you place them will determine the cooking temperature inside a Dutch oven. Experiment with your own gear to find the methods that work best for you. The pointers on pages 33–35 will help you get started, but remember to monitor cooking and adjust the heat up or down as needed.

Dutch oven pointers

Camp-style Dutch oven (three legs): To *boil, fry, brown* or *sauté* food, use the Dutch oven without a lid. Set the pot directly on a spread or cooking ring of hot coals so all the heat comes from the bottom. The legs hold the pot slightly above the coals to avoid burning. More coals equals more heat.

To *bake, roast* or *simmer* food in a Dutch oven, you need heat from both the bottom and top. Top heat promotes browning. Arrange some hot coals in a cooking ring underneath the covered pot and place more hot coals on the lid, either in rings or scattered evenly. For general cooking and most baking, place about ⅓ of the coals in the ring under the pot and about ⅔ of the coals on the lid. (Avoid placing any coals under the center of the pot or baked items may burn.) For roasting, split the coals evenly between the bottom and top. For simmering, place more coals underneath than on top.

Kitchen-style Dutch oven (flat bottom): Place this Dutch oven on a grate over hot coals (or gas grill heat) or on a gas burner.* It may also be hung over a fire on a hook or tripod by the long wire handle. To use this Dutch oven directly on hot coals, you'll need to prop it up on rocks or bricks to lift the bottom off the heat.

A propane burner may be used like a stovetop burner.

Coals: How Hot & How Many?

To cook at 325°F, double the diameter of the Dutch oven you're using (measured in inches) and use that number of standard charcoal briquettes.

- For a 10" oven, use 20 coals (10 x 2)
- For a 12" oven, use 24 coals (12 x 2)

Hotter? Every time you add two more hot coals, the temperature in the Dutch oven increases by about 25°F. So to cook at 350°F in a 10" pot, use about 22 coals; to cook at 400°F, use about 26 coals.

Cooler? Every time you remove two hot coals, the temperature goes down by about 25°F. So to cook at 300°F in a 10" pot, use about 18 coals.

If you don't want to count coals, use this quick method for any size Dutch oven: For 325°F to 350°F, make a ring of touching briquettes underneath the pot (leave space for legs). Make another ring of touching briquettes around the outer edge of the lid. To adjust the temperature up or down, add or remove coals as needed, maintaining evenly spaced rings.

FOLLOWING THE RECIPES	
If it says…	**It means…**
24+ hot coals	Start with 24 hot charcoal briquettes, but light extras to complete the cooking.
About 24 hot coals	Use about 24 hot charcoal briquettes to complete the cooking
Cook on a grate	Start with the grate 3" to 4" above heat and adjust it up or down as needed for correct cooking temperature
Medium heat	Use medium setting on a gas grill, or judge by holding your palm above the fire for 4 seconds at about the position the food will cook (2 seconds = hot heat; 6 seconds = low heat)

TEMPERATURE CONVERSION					
	Temperature				
Diameter	**300°**	**325°**	**350°**	**375°**	**400°**
5"	8 coals	10 coals	12 coals	14 coals	16 coals
6"	10 coals	12 coals	14 coals	16 coals	18 coals
8"	14 coals	16 coals	18 coals	20 coals	22 coals
10"	18 coals	20 coals	22 coals	24 coals	26 coals
12"	22 coals	24 coals	26 coals	28 coals	30 coals
14"	26 coals	28 coals	30 coals	32 coals	34 coals
16"	30 coals	32 coals	34 coals	36 coals	38 coals

This temperature conversion chart tells you about how many coals you need to reach a certain temperature in your Dutch oven. Refer to the next page to determine how the coals should be arranged depending on the way you'd like to cook your food (roasting, baking, etc.).

Placing the coals

If you are using a 12" Dutch oven with approximately 24 coals, use the following guidelines for positioning them for the cooking temperature you need:

To sauté, fry or boil: Spread all coals underneath the pot (12 to 16 coals may be enough).

To simmer or stew: Spread about 16 coals underneath the pot and 8 coals on the lid (⅔ bottom and ⅓ top). Allow the coals to burn for 1 to 1½ hours before replenishing.

To roast: Make a cooking ring with about 12 coals underneath the pot and 12 coals on the lid (½ bottom and ½ top). Replenish the coals after 30 to 45 minutes or as needed.

To bake: Make a cooking ring with about 8 coals underneath the pot and 16 coals on the lid (⅓ bottom and ⅔ top). Replenish the coals after 30 to 45 minutes or as needed.

BREAKFAST

What better way to start your day than with a hearty breakfast prepared in your favorite cast ion cookware? The nonstick surface is great for eggs, casseroles and frittatas, and you can take advantage of a deep Dutch oven to make extra-thick puffed pancakes and French toast bakes. After you've enjoyed a warm, delicious breakfast, you'll be ready to take on the day!

ZIPPY SCRAMBLED EGGS

Serve promptly with toast, muffins or pastries as desired.

Ingredients
- 12 eggs
- 1 red onion
- 1 jalapeño pepper
- ¼ C. butter
- Salt and pepper to taste
- 8 oz. firm goat cheese, crumbled
- 2 T. finely chopped fresh chives
- Toast, muffins and/or pastries, optional

Preparation
In a medium bowl, lightly beat eggs and set aside. Finely chop onion to measure ¾ cup. Slice jalapeño into thin rounds, keeping seeds as desired.

On the Stove

Place skillet on stovetop over medium-high heat and melt butter. Add onion and jalapeño; sauté until tender. Stir in eggs and season with salt and pepper. Continue to cook and stir until soft curds form or to desired doneness. Remove skillet from heat and stir in cheese and chives.

Alternate Cooking Method
Use a griddle in place of a skillet.

Variations
- Substitute other types of cheese such as Pepper Jack, Monterey Jack or cheddar.
- Add other diced vegetables such as bell pepper, cooked broccoli or mushrooms.

Over the Fire or on the Grill (About 24 hot coals)

Place skillet on a grate over medium heat (hot coals or gas grill) and melt butter. Add onion and jalapeño; sauté until tender. Stir in eggs and season with salt and pepper. Continue to cook and stir until soft curds form or to desired doneness. Remove skillet from heat and stir in cheese and chives.

SIMPLE DUTCH OVEN OMELET

Ingredients
- 10 large eggs
- 2 C. milk
- 1 C. grated Parmesan cheese
- 1 C. diced cooked ham
- ¼ C. finely chopped fresh flat-leaf parsley
- 1 tsp. salt
- Freshly ground black pepper

Preparation
Beat the eggs in a large bowl and whisk in the milk. Stir in the cheese, diced ham and parsley. Season with the salt and pepper.

On the Stove and in the Oven
Preheat oven to 375°F. Meanwhile, place Dutch oven on stovetop over medium heat. Lightly grease the oven with olive oil if you like. When hot, pour egg mixture into Dutch oven. Transfer to center rack in oven to bake uncovered for 45 minutes or until the top is slightly golden and a knife inserted in the middle comes out clean. Let cool for 5 minutes before slicing. Serve hot.

Over the Fire (28 hot coals)
Preheat and oil Dutch oven to 375°F using 11 coals under the oven and 17 coals on the lid. This will brown the top of the omelet. When hot, pour egg mixture into the Dutch oven. Bake for 45 minutes or until the top is slightly golden and a knife inserted in the middle comes out clean. When you see steam coming out from under the lid, you know it is done. Let cool for 5 minutes before slicing. Serve hot.

SIZZLIN' SKILLET
BREAKFAST

Ingredients

- 1 red bell pepper, cored, seeded
- 1 onion
- 1 clove garlic
- 1 T. butter
- 2 T. vegetable oil
- 3 C. frozen shredded hash browns, firmly packed
- ¾ tsp. salt, divided
- 6 eggs
- ¼ tsp. pepper
- ½ C. shredded cheddar or American cheese
- ¼ C. bacon bits, optional

Preparation

Dice bell pepper and onion; combine in a bowl. Mince garlic.

On the Stove

Preheat oven to 350°F. Meanwhile, place skillet on stovetop over medium heat. Add butter and oil. When hot, add bell pepper and onion; sauté until tender. Add garlic and cook for 1 minute. Stir in hash browns and ½ teaspoon salt; cover with lid and cook for 10 minutes, stirring often, until potatoes are golden brown and tender.

Remove from heat and use the back of a spoon to make six indentations in potato mixture. Break one egg into each indentation. Sprinkle eggs with pepper and remaining ¼ teaspoon salt. Reduce heat to low, cover skillet and cook for 8 to 10 minutes, until eggs are set and reach desired doneness.

Remove from heat and sprinkle with cheese and bacon bits, if desired. Cover and let stand just until cheese is melted. Serve promptly with toast.

10"
with lid

Over the Fire or on the Grill (20+ hot coals)

Place skillet on a grate over medium heat (hot coals or gas grill); add butter and oil. When hot, add bell pepper and onion; sauté until tender. Add garlic and cook for 1 minute. Stir in hash browns and ½ teaspoon salt; cover with lid and cook for 10 minutes, stirring often, until potatoes are golden brown and tender.

Remove from heat and use the back of a spoon to make six indentations in potato mixture. Break one egg into each indentation. Sprinkle eggs with pepper and remaining ¼ teaspoon salt. Cover skillet and move over indirect medium-low heat to cook for 15 to 20 minutes, until eggs are set and reach desired doneness.

Remove from heat and sprinkle with cheese and bacon bits, if desired. Cover and let stand just until cheese is melted. Serve promptly with toast.

HUNGRY CAMPER'S
BREAKFAST STRATA

SERVES
8

Ingredients
> 1 (1 lb.) loaf white bread
> 12 eggs
> 3 T. milk
> Salt and pepper to taste

> 1 lb. ground breakfast sausage
> 2 C. shredded Colby Jack cheese

Preparation
Tear or cut bread into 1" to 2" pieces; set aside. In a medium bowl, whisk together eggs, milk, salt and pepper; set aside.

★★★★ DUTCH OVEN DETAILS ★★★★

Plan Ahead

Cook sausage ahead of time and refrigerate until use. Then simply grease pot with nonstick cooking spray before adding bread and other ingredients.

On the Stove and in the Oven

Preheat oven to 350°F. Meanwhile, place Dutch oven on stovetop over medium heat; crumble sausage into pot and cook thoroughly, about 8 minutes, stirring frequently. Drain well and remove sausage to bowl, leaving thin coating of drippings in pot.

Place bread pieces in Dutch oven; top with cooked sausage. Pour prepared egg mixture evenly over bread and sausage. Cover Dutch oven and transfer to center rack in oven to bake for 30 minutes.

Remove from oven, uncover and sprinkle with cheese; replace lid and return to oven for 15 to 20 minutes more. Serve promptly.

Over the Fire (22+ hot coals)

Arrange about ½ hot coals in cooking ring underneath Dutch oven. Add sausage and cook thoroughly, stirring frequently. Drain well and remove sausage to a bowl, leaving a thin coating of drippings in the pot.

Place bread pieces in Dutch oven; top with cooked sausage. Pour prepared egg mixture evenly over bread and sausage. Cover Dutch oven. Remove several hot coals from cooking ring underneath pot to reduce heat and transfer them to the lid; place all remaining hot coals on lid. Cook about 30 minutes, rotating pot and lid twice during cooking.

Carefully remove lid and sprinkle cheese over eggs. Replace lid and cook for 15 to 20 minutes more, replenishing coals on top and bottom as needed to maintain cooking temperature. Serve promptly.

Variation
Add other ingredients as desired, such as sliced mushrooms, diced bell peppers, jalapeños or chopped onion.

HEARTY BREAKFAST PIZZA

SERVES 6-8

Ingredients

- 6 brown-and-serve sausage links, sliced
- ½ C. diced red onion
- 1 (6.5 oz.) pkg. pizza dough crust mix (plus water as directed)
- ½ C. diced Canadian bacon
- ½ C. diced ham
- ¾ C. diced yellow bell pepper
- 1½ C. frozen shredded hash browns, partially thawed
- 1½ C. shredded Italian 5-cheese blend
- 3 eggs
- 3 T. milk
- Garlic powder and black pepper to taste
- Parmesan cheese

Preparation

In a bowl, whisk together eggs, milk, garlic powder and pepper. Prepare pizza dough with water following package directions.

On the Stove and in the Oven

Preheat oven to 350°F. Meanwhile, place Dutch oven on stovetop over medium heat. Cook the sausage and onion until meat is brown and onion is tender. Remove from heat and transfer meat mixture to a bowl.

Let the Dutch oven cool and then wipe out excess grease. Line the Dutch oven with foil and grease lightly. Press pizza dough over the bottom and at least ½" up the sides of pot to form a rim. Sprinkle the sausage mixture, Canadian bacon, ham, bell pepper, hash browns and cheese blend over crust.

Pour egg mixture evenly over the ingredients inside the crust. Sprinkle with Parmesan cheese. Transfer to center rack in oven to bake uncovered for 20 to 30 minutes or until crust is golden brown on the bottom and eggs are set. Lift foil to remove pizza from pot; slice and serve.

Over the Fire (25 hot coals)

Spread about 25 hot coals in a flat layer under the Dutch oven. Cook the sausage and onion until meat is brown and onion is tender. Remove from heat and transfer meat mixture to a bowl.

Let pot cool and then wipe out excess grease. Line the pot with foil and grease lightly. Press pizza dough over the bottom and at least ½" up the sides of pot to form a rim. Sprinkle the sausage mixture, Canadian bacon, ham, bell pepper, hash browns and cheese blend over crust. Pour egg mixture evenly over the ingredients inside the crust. Sprinkle with Parmesan cheese and cover pot with lid.

Set the Dutch oven on a ring of 8 hot coals and place about 17 coals on the lid. Bake 20 to 30 minutes or until crust is golden brown on the bottom and eggs are set. Rotate pot and lid twice during cooking. Move several coals from the bottom to the center of lid during the last 5 minutes to increase browning on top. Lift foil to remove pizza from pot; slice and serve.

WAKE-UP WESTERN EGGS

Serve promptly by spooning hot egg mixture into pita pockets and topping with cheese and salsa, if desired.

Ingredients

- 6 medium pita bread rounds
- 1 onion
- 1 clove garlic
- 1 green bell pepper, cored, seeded
- 1 red bell pepper, cored, seeded
- 12 eggs
- 1 lb. ground sausage
- Shredded Pepper Jack cheese
- Salsa, optional

Preparation

Slice pita rounds in half crosswise to make 12 pockets; cover until needed. Mince onion and garlic; dice bell peppers. Set all vegetables aside. In a medium bowl, beat eggs well.

On the Stove

Place Dutch oven on stovetop over medium heat; add sausage and cook until lightly browned and crumbly, stirring frequently. Add onion, garlic and bell pepper to pot; sauté with sausage until tender. Add eggs, sprinkle with cheese as desired and scramble with a fork while cooking to desired doneness.

Over the Fire (15+ hot coals)

Spread the hot coals in a flat layer underneath Dutch oven. Add sausage and cook until lightly browned and crumbly, stirring frequently. Add onion, garlic and bell pepper to pot; sauté with sausage until tender. Add eggs, sprinkle with cheese as desired and scramble well while cooking to desired doneness. Adjust the number of coals as needed for even cooking.

Alternate Cooking Method

Use a kitchen-style Dutch oven or large skillet and cook on a grate over medium-high heat (hot coals or gas grill).

HOT & CHEESY BREAKFAST SANDWICH

Serve with marinara or ranch dressing.

Ingredients

> Butter
> Potato bread
> Green onions
> Cheddar cheese
> Mozzarella cheese
> Cooked bacon
> Pickled banana peppers, drained

Directions

Butter one bread slice; set in a pie iron, butter side down. Slice green onions; add to bread with as much cheese and bacon as you'd like. Slice peppers and toss them on before adding another bread slice, butter side up. Close the iron and cut off the extra bread. Toast in hot coals until nice and brown on both sides.

FILLED BREAKFAST BISCUITS

SERVES 5

Ingredients
- 1 can refrigerated jumbo butter-flavored biscuits
- 12 eggs
- 12 sausage patties or links
- Cheese, optional

Preparation
Scramble eggs and cook sausage and set aside.

On the Stove and in the Oven
Preheat oven to 325°F. Meanwhile, place Dutch oven on stovetop over medium heat and oil it. Pull apart one biscuit and put half in bottom of oven. Place some egg and sausage on top of biscuit then cover with other half. Repeat with remaining biscuits until bottom of Dutch oven is full. Transfer Dutch oven to center rack in oven to bake uncovered until biscuits are done. At the last minute, add cheese if desired.

Over the Fire (About 24 hot coals)
Preheat and oil the Dutch oven over a few hot coals. Pull apart one biscuit and put half in bottom of oven. Place some egg and sausage on top of biscuit then cover with other half. Repeat with remaining biscuits until bottom of Dutch oven is full. Set the Dutch oven on a ring of 8 hot coals and place about 16 coals on the lid. Bake until biscuits are done, rotating pot and lid twice during cooking. You will see steam coming out from under the lid, and you will smell it too! At the last minute, add cheese if desired.

TOASTED BAGEL SANDWICHES

Ingredients

- Bagel thins
- Precooked eggs
- Salt & pepper
- American cheese
- Canadian bacon

Directions

Set bagel halves inside a greased pie iron. Place egg on one side and sprinkle with salt and pepper. Layer on cheese and Canadian bacon. Keep the cheese in the middle so it doesn't melt through the hole in the bagel. Close the iron and hold in hot coals until the bagel has browned up nicely. The cheese will be hot and melty.

> **Variation:** Swiss cheese would be yummy, too!

COUNTRY SAUSAGE GRAVY

Serve hot gravy over biscuits or buttered toast. This gravy can also be served over mashed or fried potatoes.

Ingredients

- ½ onion
- 4 bacon strips
- 1 lb. ground breakfast sausage
- ¼ C. flour
- 2 C. milk
- ½ tsp. pepper
- ¼ tsp. garlic powder
- Biscuits (recipes on pages 68 and 70)

Preparation

Dice onion and cut bacon into small pieces.

On the Stove

Place Dutch oven on stovetop over medium heat and add sausage, bacon and onion. Cook, stirring frequently, until meat is browned and onion is tender. Do not drain off fat. Add flour and stir until blended and bubbly. Gradually whisk in 2 cups water, milk, pepper and garlic powder. Heat to simmering but do not boil.

For thicker gravy, stir in more flour, a little at a time.

Over the Fire or on the Grill (About 20 hot coals)

Place Dutch oven on a grate over medium heat (hot coals or gas grill). Add sausage, bacon and onion; cook, stirring frequently, until meat is browned and onion is tender. Do not drain. Add flour and stir until blended and bubbly. Gradually whisk in 2 cups water, milk, pepper and garlic powder. Heat to simmering, but do not boil. Adjust the number of coals as needed for even cooking.

For thicker gravy, stir in more flour, a little at a time.

LOADED HASH BROWNS

PIE IRON RECIPE

Ingredients

- 2 C. frozen shredded hash browns, thawed
- 1 egg
- Green onions
- Cooked bacon
- Cheddar cheese
- Garlic salt
- Black pepper

Directions

Grease a pie iron. Mix potatoes and egg. Add some chopped green onions and bacon; stir in some cheese. Pack potato mixture tightly into one side of your iron. Sprinkle with garlic salt and pepper. Close the pie iron and set in warm coals until toasted on one side; flip until brown on the other side and heated all the way through. A little sour cream is a nice addition to piping-hot potatoes.

> **Tip:** You can even use a separate pie iron to heat up precooked sausages. Garnish if you'd like.

APPLE-CRANBERRY PUFFED PANCAKE

Serve warm or at room temperature, drizzled with syrup if desired.

SERVES 6

Ingredients

- 1 large apple (such as Granny Smith)
- ⅔ C. flour
- 2 T. sugar
- ½ tsp. ground cinnamon
- ⅛ tsp. ground nutmeg
- Dash of salt
- 4 eggs
- 1 C. milk
- 1 tsp. vanilla extract
- ½ C. dried sweetened cranberries
- ¼ C. butter
- Powdered sugar
- Maple or berry syrup, optional

Preparation

Peel, core and thinly slice apple; set aside. In a medium bowl, mix flour, sugar, cinnamon, nutmeg and salt. In another bowl, whisk together eggs, milk and vanilla to blend. Add egg mixture to flour mixture and whisk until smooth. Stir in cranberries.

10"

In the Oven

Preheat oven to 425°F. Place butter in skillet and set skillet on center rack in oven until butter is melted. Remove skillet from oven and brush butter over bottom and sides of pan. Arrange apple slices over butter and return skillet to oven for 5 minutes or until apple slices begin to soften.

Pour prepared batter over apples. Bake uncovered for 18 to 20 minutes or until puffed and golden brown around edges and set in center. Cool slightly before sprinkling with powdered sugar. Cut into wedges to serve.

Variation

Mix 3 tablespoons sugar with ½ teaspoon ground cinnamon and sprinkle on top of batter before baking.

10"
with lid

Over the Fire (About 30 hot coals)

Arrange about ⅓ hot coals in cooking ring underneath Dutch oven. Place butter in pot. When melted, brush over bottom and sides of pot. Arrange apple slices over bottom and cover Dutch oven with lid; cook for 5 minutes or until apple slices begin to soften.

Pour prepared batter over apples. Cover and place remaining hot coals on lid. Bake for 15 to 25 minutes or until puffed and golden brown around edges and set in center. Rotate pot and lid once during cooking and adjust the number of coals on top and bottom as needed for even heat. Cool slightly before sprinkling with powdered sugar. Cut into wedges to serve.

FILLED PANCAKE ROLL-UPS

Spoon on sweet or savory filling and roll up. Garnish with whipped cream, syrup, honey or salsa as desired.

SERVES 6

Ingredients
- 1 ½ C. milk
- 3 eggs
- ½ tsp. vanilla extract
- 1 C. flour
- ¼ tsp. salt
- 1 tsp. sugar
- Butter

- Sweet or savory fillings as desired (berries, jam, diced ham, cooked sausage, shredded cheese and/ or cooked vegetables)
- Whipped cream, flavored syrup, honey or salsa, optional

Preparation
In a large bowl, whisk together milk, eggs and vanilla. Add flour, salt and sugar, blending until smooth.

10"

On the Stove and in the Oven

Preheat oven to 200°F. Meanwhile, place skillet on stovetop over medium-high heat and melt 1 to 2 teaspoons butter; spread evenly over bottom of pan. Pour ¼ cup prepared batter into skillet and tilt pan so batter spreads out thinly and evenly. Cook until top looks dry, about 30 seconds. Carefully flip pancake with a spatula; cook on other side for several seconds, until golden brown.

Repeat to make additional pancakes with remaining batter. Place prepared pancakes on a cookie sheet and cover with foil; place in oven to keep warm.

10"

Over the Fire or on the Grill (About 20 hot coals)

Place skillet on a grate over medium heat (hot coals or gas grill) and melt 1 to 2 teaspoons butter; spread evenly over bottom of pan. Pour ¼ cup prepared batter into skillet and tilt pan so batter spreads out thinly and evenly. Cook until top looks dry, about 30 seconds. Carefully flip pancake with a spatula; cook on other side for several seconds, until golden brown. Adjust the number and placement of coals as needed for even cooking.

Repeat to make additional pancakes with remaining batter. Wrap pancakes in foil and set over indirect heat to keep warm.

Alternate Cooking Method
Use a griddle in place of a skillet. Spread out batter with a large spoon.

FIRESIDE APPLESAUCE PANCAKES

Ingredients

- ½ tsp. lemon juice
- ¼ C. milk
- 1 C. biscuit baking mix
- ½ tsp. cinnamon
- 1 egg
- ½ C. applesauce

Directions

Combine baking mix, cinnamon, egg, applesauce, lemon juice and milk. Stir until the lumps are nearly gone. Fill one side of a greased pie iron with batter. Hold level while cooking in warm coals; don't flip iron until you've peeked inside and the batter has thickened up nicely. Cook until both sides are brown. Serve with syrup and applesauce.

HEARTY CORNMEAL PANCAKES

SERVES 4

Ingredients

- ½ C. flour
- ½ C. whole wheat flour
- ½ C. cornmeal
- 2 T. sugar
- 1 ¼ tsp. baking powder
- ½ tsp. baking soda
- 1 tsp. salt

- 1 ½ C. buttermilk
- ¼ C. milk
- 3 T. butter, melted and cooled
- 1 egg, lightly beaten
- Additional butter
- Syrup (recipes on page 59)

Preparation

In a medium bowl, stir together flour, whole wheat flour, cornmeal, sugar, baking powder, baking soda and salt. In a separate bowl, whisk together buttermilk, milk, melted butter and egg. Whisk milk mixture into dry ingredients until just combined (lumps will remain).

Griddle

On the Stove and in the Oven

Preheat oven to 200°F. Meanwhile, place griddle on stovetop over medium heat. When hot, grease lightly with butter. Spoon ⅓ cup prepared batter onto griddle for each pancake. Cook until edges are set, 3 to 4 minutes (bubbles will not appear as with traditional pancakes). Flip pancakes and cook until golden brown, about 2 minutes.

Repeat with remaining batter, greasing griddle as needed. Keep prepared pancakes warm on a cookie sheet in the oven.

Griddle

Over the Fire or on the Grill (About 20 hot coals)

Place griddle on grate over medium heat (hot coals or gas grill). When hot, grease lightly with butter. Spoon ⅓ cup prepared batter onto griddle for each pancake. Cook until edges are set, 3 to 4 minutes (bubbles will not appear as with traditional pancakes). Flip pancakes and cook until golden brown, about 2 minutes. Adjust the number and placement of coals as needed for even cooking.

Repeat with remaining batter, greasing griddle as needed. Stack cooked pancakes on aluminum foil, cover lightly and set over indirect heat to keep warm.

EASY FRENCH TOAST BAKE

Serve with warm syrup and fresh fruit on the side.

Ingredients
- 1 lg. loaf French bread
- 8 eggs
- 3 C. milk
- ¼ C. sugar
- 1½ tsp. ground cinnamon
- ½ tsp. salt
- 2 tsp. vanilla
- ¼ C. butter
- Syrup

Preparation
In a large bowl, whisk together eggs, milk, sugar, cinnamon, salt and vanilla until smooth.

In the Oven

Preheat oven to 325°F. Grease Dutch oven. Tear bread into 1" to 2" chunks and toss them into the pot. Pour egg mixture over the bread and stir lightly. Cut butter into small pieces and scatter over the top. Place Dutch oven on center rack in oven to bake uncovered 45 to 55 minutes or until set and golden brown around edges.

Over the Fire (About 24 hot coals)

Grease the Dutch oven. Tear bread into 1" to 2" chunks and toss them into the pot. Pour egg mixture over the bread and stir lightly. Cut butter into small pieces and scatter over the top. Cover pot with lid.

Set the Dutch oven on a ring of 9 hot coals and place about 15 coals on the lid. Bake 45 to 55 minutes or until set and golden brown around edges. Rotate pot and lid several times during baking and replenish coals as needed to maintain cooking temperature.

Variation
Try using eggnog in place of the milk and seasonings for an extra-simple, quick-fix breakfast.

This breakfast treat also makes a pretty delicious dessert. Be sure to save any leftovers!

CARAMELIZED PEACH
FRENCH TOAST

Serve warm with butter and warm syrup, if desired.

Ingredients

- 12 eggs
- 2 C. milk
- ½ tsp. vanilla extract
- 2 tsp. ground cinnamon
- 1 C. margarine
- 1 loaf French or Italian bread
- 3 (15.2 oz.) cans peach halves, drained
- 2½ C. brown sugar

Preparation

In a large bowl, whisk together eggs, milk, vanilla and cinnamon; set aside. Cut up margarine, slice bread and quarter peaches; set aside.

In the Oven

Place Dutch oven into oven as it preheats to 350°F. Meanwhile, place bread slices in egg mixture to soak. Remove Dutch oven and add margarine, stirring until melted. Stir in brown sugar to caramelize.

Arrange peaches over caramel mixture. Place soaked bread on top of peaches. Cover Dutch oven and return to oven to bake for 35 to 45 minutes or until done. Remove lid for the last 10 minutes of baking.

Over the Fire (26+ hot coals)

Place bread slices in egg mixture to soak. Meanwhile, arrange about ⅓ hot coals in cooking ring underneath Dutch oven. Put margarine in pot, cover with lid and place remaining hot coals on lid. When butter is melted and sizzling, remove Dutch oven from coals and carefully take off lid. Add brown sugar and stir until light brown and caramelized.

Arrange peaches over caramel mixture. Place soaked bread on top of peaches. Replace lid and return Dutch oven to cooking ring. Cook for 35 to 45 minutes or until done. Rotate pot and lid twice during cooking and replenish coals on top and bottom as needed to maintain cooking temperature.

STUFFED STRAWBERRY
FRENCH TOAST

Ingredients

> Eggs
> Milk
> Cinnamon/sugar
> White bread
> Strawberry jelly or jam

Directions

Spray a pie iron with cooking spray. Mix eggs, milk and cinnamon/sugar like you normally would for French toast. Dip one side of bread in egg and set in iron, egg side down. Spread jelly on top. Dip another bread slice in egg and place it on top, egg side up. Close the iron and cook in hot coals to toast the bread.

BREADS

Warm, fluffy, airy. At its most essential, bread is nothing more than the combination of flour, water, and heat. But anyone who has smelled baking bread and couldn't help but steer toward it knows that bread does one thing better than almost anything else: it brings people together. Breaking bread has always meant hospitality. The recipes that follow range from quick-and-easy rolls to rustic loaves. No matter what bread you bake, however, it'll make you good company!

BACON LOVER'S BREAD

SERVES 10

Ingredients
- 12 frozen unbaked dinner rolls, thawed but still cold
- 3 T. butter, melted
- 6 bacon strips, cooked and crumbled
- 1 C. shredded cheddar, Swiss, or Colby-Jack cheese

Preparation
Cut each dinner roll into 3 pieces and coat in melted butter.

In the Oven

Preheat oven to 375°F. Meanwhile, line Dutch oven with foil. Arrange dinner roll pieces evenly in pot. Sprinkle bacon and cheese over the top. Cover pot with lid and let dough rise until double in size, about 2 hours.

Uncover and place Dutch oven on center rack in oven to bake 25 to 35 minutes or until golden brown on top and bottom and no longer doughy in the center.

Over the Fire (About 24 hot coals)

Line Dutch oven with foil. Arrange dinner roll pieces evenly in pot. Sprinkle bacon and cheese over the top. Cover pot with lid and let dough rise until double in size, about 2 hours.

To bake, set the Dutch oven on a ring of 8 hot coals and arrange about 16 coals on the lid. Bake 25 to 35 minutes or until golden brown on top and bottom and no longer doughy in the center. Rotate pot and lid twice during baking and rearrange coals as needed to maintain cooking temperature and promote browning on top.

CAMPSITE BISCUITS

Ingredients
- 2 ½ C. self-rising flour, divided
- ½ to ¾ tsp. salt
- 1 ½ T. sugar
- 2 T. shortening
- 2 T. butter, softened
- 1 ¼ C. buttermilk
- 1 ½ T. butter, melted

Preparation
In a bowl, combine 2 cups flour, salt and sugar. Cut in shortening and soft butter until pea-size crumbs form. Stir in buttermilk until incorporated, but don't over-mix (dough will be very wet). Let dough rest 2 to 3 minutes.

In the Oven
Preheat oven to 400°F. Meanwhile, lightly oil Dutch oven. Place remaining ½ cup flour in a bowl and grease a large spoon. For each biscuit, drop a spoonful of dough into the flour. With floured hands, shape dough into a soft ball, shaking off excess flour. Set in oiled pot. Repeat to make a single layer of biscuits. Drizzle with melted butter. Place Dutch oven on center rack in oven to bake uncovered 20 to 30 minutes.

Over the Fire (About 26 hot coals)
Lightly oil Dutch oven. Place remaining ½ cup flour in a bowl and grease a large spoon. For each biscuit, drop a spoonful of dough into the flour. With floured hands, shape dough into a soft ball, shaking off excess flour. Set in oiled pot. Repeat to make a single layer of biscuits. Drizzle with melted butter and cover pot with lid.

Set the Dutch oven on a ring of 7 hot coals and place about 19 coals on the lid. Bake 20 to 30 minutes, rotating pot and lid twice during cooking. Move several coals to the center of lid near the end of cooking time to promote browning.

Tip: Short on time? Try baking refrigerated biscuit dough in a greased 8" round metal baking pan set on a riser inside the Dutch oven. Ready in 10 to 20 minutes!

For a sweet treat, use honey to top these biscuits.

SPICY YAM BISCUITS

Serve warm or at room temperature with butter and/or honey as desired.

Ingredients

> 2 ¼ C. flour
> 1 T. baking powder
> 1 tsp. salt
> 1 tsp. sugar
> ¼ tsp. chili powder, or to taste
> ⅛ tsp. cayenne pepper, or to taste
> ½ C. butter, sliced
> ½ C. drained, mashed canned yams
> ¾ C. buttermilk or half-and-half
> Butter and/or honey, optional

Preparation

In a medium bowl, mix flour, baking powder, salt, sugar, chili powder and cayenne pepper. With a pastry blender or two knives, cut in butter until mixture is crumbly. Stir in yams and buttermilk until dough holds together.

Place dough on a well-floured surface and knead lightly several times. Roll out dough to ¾" thickness. Cut biscuits with round cookie cutter, drinking glass or empty soup can from which both ends have been removed.

★★★★ DUTCH OVEN DETAILS ★★★★

Creative Cooking

Food can be cooked directly in a Dutch oven or in a secondary pan set on a "riser" inside so the Dutch oven acts like a standard oven. To make a riser, place several metal nuts, clean pebbles, balls of foil or an inverted metal pie plate or canning jar ring inside the Dutch oven and set the baking pan of food on top. Cover the pot with a lid. See page 95 for an illustration.

In the Oven

Preheat oven to 400°F. Generously grease bottom of skillet with nonstick cooking spray. Arrange biscuits close together in a single layer in skillet. Bake uncovered for 18 to 23 minutes or until golden brown.

Over the Fire (About 30 hot coals)

Generously grease bottom of Dutch oven with nonstick cooking spray. Arrange about ⅓ hot coals in cooking ring and set Dutch oven on top for 10 minutes to preheat.

Arrange biscuits in a single layer in Dutch oven. Cover pot and place remaining hot coals on lid. Cook for 15 to 20 minutes or until biscuits are golden brown. Rotate pot and lid once during cooking and transfer most of the hot coals from bottom ring to lid toward end of cooking time to promote browning on top.

Variation
Substitute mashed baked sweet potato flesh for the canned yams.

VINTAGE SPOTLIGHT

Combined Gridiron and Spider, U.S. Patent No. 78, dated 11/14/1836. This piece was used as both a broiler and a skillet on hot coals raked from the fireplace onto the hearth.

ITALIAN PESTO ROLLS

Serve warm or at room temperature.

Ingredients

- 1 (16 oz.) pkg. Pillsbury Hot Roll Mix
- 2 T. plus ¼ C. butter, softened, divided
- 1 egg
- ⅔ C. grated Parmesan cheese
- 1½ tsp. garlic powder
- 2 tsp. Italian seasoning
- ½ tsp. dried oregano
- Flour for kneading
- Sun-dried tomato pesto

Preparation

Following directions on roll mix package, mix contents of box and yeast in a large bowl. Stir in 1 cup hot water, 2 tablespoons butter and egg until dough forms. On floured surface, shape dough into a ball and knead until smooth, about 5 minutes. Cover dough with large bowl and let rest 5 minutes. Meanwhile, in a small bowl, stir together Parmesan cheese, garlic powder, Italian seasoning and oregano; set aside.

Roll dough into an 8" x 18" rectangle. Spread remaining ¼ cup butter and pesto over dough. Sprinkle evenly with cheese mixture. Starting at one long edge, roll up dough cinnamon-roll fashion and pinch long edge to seal. Cut into rolls about 1½" thick.

In the Oven

Grease bottom and lower sides of Dutch oven with nonstick cooking spray. Arrange rolls in a single layer in pot; cover with a cloth and let rise in a warm place until doubled in size, 30 to 40 minutes.

Preheat oven to 350°F. Remove cloth and bake uncovered for 25 to 30 minutes or until lightly browned. Allow rolls to cool in oven for several minutes before removing.

Tip
Use thread or unflavored dental floss to slice rolls easily and maintain round shape.

Over the Fire (About 26 hot coals)

Grease bottom of Dutch oven with nonstick cooking spray and arrange rolls in a single layer in pot. Cover with lid and let rise in a warm place until doubled in size, 30 to 40 minutes.

Arrange about ⅓ hot coals in cooking ring underneath Dutch oven and place remaining hot coals on lid. Cook for 18 to 25 minutes or until lightly browned. Rotate pot and lid twice during cooking and transfer most of the hot coals from bottom ring to lid toward end of cooking time to promote browning on top. Allow rolls to cool in oven for several minutes before removing.

Alternate Cooking Method
This recipe may also be baked in a 12" cast iron skillet.

SWEET DUTCH OVEN CORNBREAD

Serve wedges with butter, jam, jelly and/or honey.

SERVES 8

Ingredients

- 1 C. cornmeal
- 1 C. flour
- ½ C. sugar
- ¼ tsp. baking soda
- 1 T. baking powder
- 1 tsp. salt
- 2 eggs, lightly beaten
- 1 ½ C. buttermilk
- ½ C. butter, melted
- Vegetable oil
- Butter, jam, jelly and/or honey

Preparation

In a medium bowl, stir together cornmeal, flour, sugar, baking soda, baking powder and salt. In another bowl, whisk together eggs and buttermilk. Add buttermilk mixture to cornmeal mixture and stir until blended. Stir in melted butter.

★★★★ DUTCH OVEN DETAILS ★★★★

Do the Twist

Rotating the Dutch oven pot and lid is especially important when baking breads. It promotes even browning and prevents burn spots.

In the Oven

Preheat oven to 400°F. Brush bottom and lower sides of Dutch oven with oil. Spread prepared batter in Dutch oven and bake uncovered for 20 to 25 minutes or until lightly browned and firm in center. Let cool slightly before removing to a plate. Slice in wedges to serve.

Over the Fire (About 26 hot coals)

Brush bottom and lower sides of Dutch oven with oil. Arrange about ⅓ hot coals in cooking ring and set Dutch oven on top for several minutes to preheat.

Spread prepared batter in hot pot. Cover and place remaining hot coals on lid. Bake for 15 to 25 minutes or until lightly browned and firm in center. Rotate pot and lid twice during cooking and transfer several coals from bottom ring to lid toward end of cooking time to promote even browning. Let cool slightly before removing to a plate. Slice in wedges to serve.

Alternate Cooking Method
This recipe may also be baked in a 10" cast iron skillet.

VINTAGE SPOTLIGHT

Stovetop Broiler, circa 1850. To use this cast iron piece, the lids of the wood stove were removed to expose the fire box. The ribs of the broiler are concave to guide juices to the center section so they could be saved.

SKILLET-BAKED SOUTHERN CORNBREAD

Serve warm or at room temperature with butter and/or honey.

Ingredients
- 2 C. cornmeal
- ½ C. flour
- 1 tsp. baking powder
- 1 tsp. salt
- 1 egg, lightly beaten
- 2 C. buttermilk
- 3 T. warm bacon drippings (or vegetable oil), divided
- Butter and/or honey

Preparation
In a medium bowl, stir together cornmeal, flour, baking powder and salt; set aside. In another bowl, whisk together egg, buttermilk and 2 tablespoons bacon drippings. Pour buttermilk mixture into cornmeal mixture and stir to blend.

In the Oven
Preheat oven to 400°F. Place remaining 1 tablespoon bacon drippings in skillet and set skillet in oven for 2 to 3 minutes until sizzling. Remove skillet from oven and swirl pan to coat bottom and sides.

Spread prepared batter in hot skillet and return to oven; bake uncovered for 20 to 25 minutes or until cornbread is lightly browned and pulls away from sides of skillet. Cool slightly before removing from pan. Slice into wedges.

Alternate Cooking Method
Use a 10" camp-style Dutch oven on a ring of hot coals, with ⅔ of the coals on the lid. No flipping required.

Variation
Stir bacon bits, chopped jalapeños, hot sauce or cayenne pepper into batter before baking to kick up the flavor.

10"
with lid

Over the Fire or on the Grill (About 26 hot coals)

Place grate over medium-high heat (hot coals or gas grill). Place remaining tablespoon bacon drippings in skillet and set on grate to preheat. When sizzling, swirl skillet to coat bottom and sides.

Spread batter in hot skillet; partially cover with lid. Spread out about ½ hot coals and push remaining coals to one side or move skillet over indirect heat. Cook until top is dry, bottom is lightly browned and bread is set, about 25 minutes. Rotate skillet several times for even heat. Remove lid and carefully flip cornbread over in skillet; cook uncovered about 10 minutes more or until lightly browned on other side. Cool slightly before removing from skillet. Slice into wedges.

CHEESY JALAPEÑO
MONKEY BREAD

SERVES
8

Ingredients

- 2 (7.5 oz.) tubes refrigerated country-style biscuits
- 8 oz. cream cheese
- 3 T. butter
- 1 C. shredded cheddar cheese
- ¾ C. canned sliced jalapeños

Preparation

Remove biscuits from tubes. With kitchen shears, cut each biscuit into four equal pieces. Cut cream cheese into cubes.

★★★★ SKILLET SECRETS ★★★★

The Perfect Find

With its rising popularity, new cast iron cookware is easy to find direct from manufacturers and even at your local department store. If you're looking for a vintage piece or are a bargain hunter, don't worry, there are still plenty of options for you.

Thrift and antique stores are great places to find vintage cookware, but many store owners are becoming aware of the popularity of older cast iron pieces, so you might find the prices to be a little higher than anticipated. If this is the case, try a garage sale, where you can often talk down the price, especially if the piece is rusty (a problem easily solved once you get it home). Ebay is also an excellent resource, as you can search for vintage cookware by brand and price.

On the Stove and in the Oven

Preheat oven to 375°F. Meanwhile, place skillet on stovetop over medium-low heat. Add butter and stir until melted. Remove skillet from heat and stir in cheddar cheese and jalapeños.

Add biscuit pieces to cheese mixture and toss until well coated. Arrange half the biscuit pieces evenly in skillet. Sprinkle evenly with cream cheese pieces. Top with remaining biscuit pieces. Place skillet on center rack in oven and bake uncovered for 10 to 15 minutes or until lightly browned. Let cool 1 minute and then carefully invert biscuits onto a lightly greased platter.

Over the Fire or on the Grill (About 22 hot coals)

Arrange about ⅓ hot coals in cooking ring underneath Dutch oven. Add butter and stir until melted. Remove pot from heat and stir in cheddar cheese and jalapeños.

Add biscuit pieces to cheese mixture and toss until well coated. Arrange half the biscuit pieces evenly in bottom of Dutch oven. Sprinkle evenly with cream cheese pieces. Top with remaining biscuit pieces. Cover pot with lid. Return Dutch oven to cooking ring and place remaining hot coals on lid. Cook for 10 to 17 minutes or until lightly browned. Rotate pot and lid once during cooking and adjust the number of coals on top and bottom as needed for even cooking. Let cool 1 minute and then carefully invert biscuits onto a lightly greased platter.

Alternate Cooking Method

Use a 10" skillet with lid and cook on a grate over medium heat (hot coals or gas grill). Rotate skillet twice during cooking and reduce heat as needed to prevent overcooking.

QUICK 'N' EASY CINNAMON ROLLS

Ingredients
- 24 frozen unbaked dinner rolls
- 1 C. brown sugar
- 5 tsp. ground cinnamon
- ½ C. chopped pecans
- ½ C. butter, melted
- ½ (16 oz.) can ready-to-use cream cheese frosting

Preparation
Line Dutch oven with foil and grease generously.

In the Oven

Preheat oven to 325°F. Arrange the balls of frozen dough in the lined pot. Sprinkle with brown sugar, cinnamon and pecans. Drizzle evenly with butter. Cover pot with lid and set aside until rolls are doubled in size, 3 to 5 hours.

Uncover and place Dutch oven on center rack in oven to bake 25 to 35 minutes or until golden brown and cooked through. Lift foil to remove rolls from Dutch oven; frost rolls or pull apart and serve with a side of frosting for dipping.

Over the Fire (About 23 hot coals)

Arrange the balls of frozen dough in the lined pot. Sprinkle with brown sugar, cinnamon and pecans. Drizzle evenly with butter. Cover pot with lid and set aside until rolls are doubled in size, 3 to 5 hours.

To bake, set the Dutch oven on a ring of 8 hot coals and place about 15 coals on the lid. Bake 25 to 35 minutes or until golden brown and cooked through. Rotate the pot and lid twice during cooking and check doneness. Move some coals from the bottom ring to the center of lid during the last 5 to 10 minutes of cooking to promote browning. Lift foil to remove rolls from Dutch oven; frost rolls or pull apart and serve with a side of frosting for dipping.

Tip: Prep these cinnamon rolls and then let them rise in the pot while you're out having fun. Bake them later for ooey gooey goodness—never easier, never tastier!

CAMPER'S FOCACCIA

Serve warm or at room temperature.

Ingredients

- 3 C. flour
- 2 tsp. yeast
- 1 tsp. sugar
- 3 to 4 tsp. dried herbs (such as basil, rosemary, thyme, dill or desired combination), divided
- ¼ C. olive oil, divided
- 1½ T. lemon juice
- 2 tsp. coarse sea salt, or to taste, divided
- ⅓ C. grated Asiago, Parmesan or Romano cheese

Preparation

In a medium bowl, mix flour, yeast and sugar. Add ¾ cup plus 2 tablespoons very warm water and stir until dough forms. Cover bowl and let rest for 15 to 20 minutes.

To dough in bowl, add 2 teaspoons herbs, 2 tablespoons olive oil, lemon juice, 1 teaspoon salt and Asiago cheese. Use hands to work ingredients into dough until well incorporated (dough will seem oily). Knead dough for 10 minutes until smooth. Cover with a cloth and let rise in a warm place until doubled in size, about 30 minutes.

In the Oven

Preheat oven to 450°F. Grease skillet with nonstick cooking spray. Pat dough evenly over bottom of skillet. With fingers, press ½"-deep indentations evenly spaced over top of dough. Brush dough with remaining 2 tablespoons oil and sprinkle with remaining 1 to 2 teaspoons herbs and 1 teaspoon salt.

Place skillet on center rack in oven and bake uncovered for 15 to 20 minutes or to desired crustiness. Cool slightly before cutting into wedges.

10"
with lid

Over the Fire (About 28 hot coals)

Grease bottom of Dutch oven with nonstick cooking spray. Pat dough evenly over bottom of pot. With fingers, press ½"-deep indentations evenly spaced over top of dough. Brush with remaining 2 tablespoons oil and sprinkle with remaining 1 to 2 teaspoons herbs and 1 teaspoon salt. Cover pot with lid.

Arrange about ⅓ hot coals in cooking ring underneath Dutch oven. Place remaining hot coals on lid. Bake for 10 to 20 minutes or to desired crustiness. Rotate pot and lid twice during cooking. Adjust the number of hot coals on top and bottom as needed for even cooking. Cool slightly before cutting into wedges.

EASY SOURDOUGH BREAD

Serve warm or at room temperature.

Ingredients
- 2 C. plain yogurt
- 1 T. yeast
- 2 T. honey
- 2 tsp. salt
- 1 T. vegetable oil
- 4⅓ to 5 C. flour

Preparation
Heat yogurt until just lukewarm. In a large bowl, combine ¼ cup very warm water with yeast; stir to dissolve. Stir in yogurt, honey, salt, oil and 2 cups flour until blended and then beat until smooth. Gradually stir in most of remaining flour, a little at a time, adding just enough to make a soft dough that pulls away from side of bowl. Turn out on floured surface and knead until smooth and elastic, about 10 minutes.

Place dough in a large greased bowl, turning once to grease the top. Cover with a cloth and let rise in a warm place until doubled in size, about 1½ hours. Punch dough down and shape into a round loaf.

In the Oven
Grease Dutch oven with nonstick cooking spray. Place shaped dough in pot, cover with lid and let rise in a warm place for 45 minutes.

Preheat oven to 375°F. Remove cloth and place pot on center rack in oven. Bake uncovered for 10 minutes; then reduce heat to 350°F. Bake 30 to 35 minutes more or until bread is golden brown and sounds hollow when tapped. Remove from Dutch oven and cool before slicing.

Variation
If desired, make several diagonal slashes in the top of the loaf before baking.

10"
with lid

Over the Fire (24+ hot coals)

Grease Dutch oven with nonstick cooking spray. Place shaped dough in pot, cover
with lid and let rise in a warm place for 45 minutes.

   Arrange about ⅓ hot coals in cooking ring underneath Dutch oven. Place
remaining hot coals on lid. Bake for 40 to 45 minutes or until bread is golden brown
and sounds hollow when tapped. Rotate pot and lid several times during cooking and
replenish coals as needed to maintain cooking temperature. To promote browning
on top, transfer most of the hot coals from bottom ring to lid toward end of cooking
time. Remove from Dutch oven to cool before slicing.

JUMBO GARLIC BREAD RING

Serve warm or at room temperature.

Ingredients

- ½ C. grated Parmesan cheese
- 1 tsp. garlic powder
- ½ tsp. onion salt
- 2 (1 lb.) loaves frozen bread dough, thawed until soft but still cold
- ⅓ C. butter, melted

Preparation

In a small bowl, mix Parmesan cheese, garlic powder and onion salt. Spread mixture on a large jellyroll pan and set aside.

Cut each loaf into four even pieces (total of eight). Use hands to stretch and form each piece into a rope about 18" long.

★★★★ ALL FIRED UP ★★★★

Get Creative with Coals

Rather than adding fresh coals near the end of cooking time, try brushing the ashes off existing coals so they'll burn hot for a while longer.

In the Oven

Grease Dutch oven with nonstick cooking spray. Brush all sides of dough rope with melted butter; roll in set-aside cheese mixture to coat. Coil rope in center of pot. Continue to coat ropes, attaching to end of previous rope to form a 10" to 11" dough circle. Cover with a cloth and let rise in a warm place until doubled in size, 30 to 40 minutes.

When ready to bake, preheat oven to 350°F. Remove cloth and bake uncovered for 30 to 35 minutes or until golden brown. Cool slightly before removing from pot.

Over the Fire (About 27 hot coals)

Grease Dutch oven with nonstick cooking spray. Brush all sides of dough rope with melted butter; roll in set-aside cheese mixture to coat. Coil rope in the center of pot. Continue to coat ropes, attaching to end of previous rope to form a 10" to 11" dough circle. Cover with lid and let rise in a warm place until doubled in size, 30 to 40 minutes.

When ready to cook, arrange about ⅓ hot coals in cooking ring underneath Dutch oven. Place remaining hot coals on lid. Cook for 25 to 35 minutes or until golden brown. Rotate pot and lid twice during cooking and transfer several coals from bottom ring to lid toward end of cooking time to promote browning. Cool slightly before removing from pot.

Variation

Jumbo Cinnamon Bread Ring: In place of cheese mixture, mix ½ cup sugar, ½ cup brown sugar and 1½ teaspoons cinnamon. Brush dough ropes with melted butter; roll in sugar mixture. Line Dutch oven with parchment paper. Coil coated dough ropes in pot; sprinkle with ½ cup chopped nuts. Let rise and bake as directed above. Cool slightly and frost with powdered sugar glaze.

CRAN-ORANGE BREAD

Ingredients

- ¾ C. sugar
- 1 (3 oz.) box vanilla cook-and-serve pudding mix (*not instant*)
- Zest and juice from 1 orange
- 2 (12 oz.) tubes refrigerated Texas-style biscuits
- ½ C. butter, melted
- ½ C. dried sweetened cranberries, divided
- 1 C. vanilla ready-to-use frosting

Preparation

In a bowl, combine the sugar, pudding mix and orange zest. Cut each biscuit into 4 pieces; dip in melted butter and roll in sugar mixture.

For glaze, mix frosting with enough orange juice to make a thin glaze.

In the Oven

Preheat oven to 375°F. Grease the Dutch oven and line it with parchment paper, if desired. Place half the biscuits in the pot and sprinkle with half the cranberries. Top with remaining biscuits and cranberries. Pour any leftover butter and sugar over the top.

Place Dutch oven on center rack in oven to bake uncovered for 15 to 25 minutes or until lightly browned. Let cool 1 minute and then invert onto a buttered platter, or glaze promptly by drizzling glaze mixture over warm biscuits and serve from pot.

Tip

Melting butter at the campsite is easy. Just place it in a metal bowl and set it over a few hot coals until it turns to liquid gold.

10"
with lid

Over the Fire (About 23 hot coals)

Grease the Dutch oven and line it with parchment paper, if desired. Place half the biscuits in the pot and sprinkle with half the cranberries. Top with remaining biscuits and cranberries. Pour any leftover butter and sugar over the top. Cover pot with lid.

Set the Dutch oven on a ring of 9 hot coals and place about 14 coals on the lid. Bake 15 to 25 minutes or until lightly browned, rotating pot and lid once. Near the end of baking time, move a few coals to the center of lid to increase browning on top. Let cool 1 minute and then invert onto a buttered platter, or glaze promptly by drizzling glaze mixture over warm biscuits and serve from pot.

AUTUMN PUMPKIN BREAD

Serve at room temperature.

Ingredients

- ½ C. brown sugar
- ½ C. chopped nuts
- ½ C. quick-cooking rolled oats
- 1 tsp. vanilla extract
- 2 T. butter
- 3⅓ C. flour
- ½ tsp. baking powder
- 1 tsp. baking soda

- 1½ tsp. salt
- 1 tsp. ground cinnamon
- 1 tsp. ground nutmeg
- 1 tsp. ground cloves
- 2 C. sugar
- 1 (15 oz.) can pumpkin
- 1 C. vegetable oil
- 4 eggs, lightly beaten

Preparation

In a medium bowl, combine brown sugar, nuts, oats, vanilla and butter. Mix until topping is crumbly.

In a large bowl, stir together flour, baking powder, baking soda, salt, cinnamon, nutmeg, cloves and sugar. Add ½ cup water, pumpkin, oil and eggs; mix batter well.

In the Oven

Preheat oven to 325°F. Grease Dutch oven with nonstick cooking spray. Pour batter into pot and sprinkle with prepared topping. Bake uncovered for 45 to 55 minutes or until bread tests done with a toothpick. Let cool before slicing.

Variation

Add 2 cups chocolate chips to batter before baking.

12" with lid

Over the Fire (24+ hot coals)

Grease Dutch oven with nonstick cooking spray. Arrange about ⅓ hot coals in cooking ring and set pot on coals to preheat for 5 to 10 minutes. Pour batter into hot Dutch oven and spread evenly; sprinkle with prepared topping.

Cover pot and place remaining hot coals on lid. Bake for 40 to 50 minutes or until bread tests done with a toothpick. Rotate pot and lid several times during cooking and replenish coals on top and bottom as needed to maintain cooking temperature. Let cool before slicing.

SWEET BUTTERSCOTCH PECAN ROLLS

Serve while warm and gooey!

Ingredients

- ½ C. butter
- ½ C. brown sugar
- 1 (3.5 oz.) pkg. cook & serve pudding mix (not instant)
- 24 frozen unbaked dinner rolls
- ½ C. chopped pecans

Preparation

In a small saucepan, combine butter, brown sugar and pudding mix.

★★★★ DUTCH OVEN DETAILS ★★★★

Wolfgang Puck Scores an A

While cast iron might bring to mind images of vintage pieces, there are plenty of new cast iron products hitting the market every day. And they're receiving the same rave reviews as their oldster counterparts. In fact, Wolfgang Puck's line of cast iron cookware received an A rating from *Good Housekeeping*.

On the Stove and in the Oven

Grease bottom of Dutch oven with nonstick cooking spray. Line bottom with a circle of parchment paper and spray paper. Arrange rolls in a single layer in pot; set aside.

Place saucepan on stovetop over medium-low heat and bring pudding mixture to a boil, stirring constantly until syrup forms. Pour syrup evenly over rolls. Sprinkle with pecans. Cover pot with a cloth and allow rolls to thaw and rise in a warm place until doubled in size, 3 to 5 hours.

When ready to bake, preheat oven to 350°F. Remove cloth and bake rolls for 25 to 30 minutes or until well browned and cooked through.

Let cool for 3 minutes and then carefully invert hot rolls onto a lightly greased heat-proof platter. Cool slightly before serving.

Over the Fire (10+ about 26 hot coals)

Generously grease bottom of Dutch oven with nonstick cooking spray. Line bottom with circle of parchment paper and spray paper. Arrange rolls in a single layer in pot; set aside.

Place saucepan on a grate over 10 hot coals and bring pudding mixture to a boil, stirring constantly until syrup forms. Pour syrup evenly over rolls. Sprinkle with pecans. Cover pot with lid and allow rolls to thaw and rise in a warm place until doubled in size, 3 to 5 hours.

When ready to cook, remove grate. Arrange about ⅓ hot coals in cooking ring underneath covered Dutch oven. Place remaining hot coals on lid. Cook for 25 to 35 minutes or until well browned and cooked through. Rotate pot and lid twice during cooking and adjust the number of coals on top and bottom as needed for even cooking.

Remove lid and let cool for 3 minutes. Carefully invert hot rolls onto a lightly greased heat-proof platter. Cool slightly before serving.

QUICK-FIX BREADS

Over the Fire (About 28 hot coals)

Refrigerated Biscuit Dough (1 tube): Prepare riser in Dutch oven (see illustration below). Grease an 8" round metal baking pan with nonstick cooking spray and arrange biscuits in a single layer in pan. Set pan on riser and cover pot with lid. Arrange about ⅓ hot coals in cooking ring underneath Dutch oven and spread remaining hot coals on lid. Bake about 10 minutes or until golden brown.

In the Oven

Frozen Dinner Rolls (8 to 10 rolls): Grease skillet with nonstick cooking spray. Place frozen rolls in skillet, cover with greased waxed paper and set in a warm place to rise for 3 to 5 hours. When doubled in size, preheat oven to 350°F and bake rolls for 15 to 20 minutes or until golden brown.

Packaged Cornbread Mix (1 package): Mix cornbread with other ingredients as directed on package. Preheat oven to 400°F. Grease skillet with nonstick cooking spray and place in oven to preheat for 10 minutes. Spread prepared batter in hot skillet and bake uncovered for 15 to 20 minutes or until light golden brown.

On the Stove

Garlic Toast (from loaf of sliced French bread): Spread both sides of bread slices with softened butter and sprinkle with garlic powder as desired. Place griddle on stovetop over medium-high heat to preheat. When hot, cook slices for 1 to 3 minutes on each side or until lightly toasted.

Alternate Cooking Method
Cook it outdoors with a griddle on grate over medium-high heat (hot coals or gas grill).

Camp-Style Dutch Oven Variation

To cook packaged cornbread over fire, use about 26 hot coals and prepare riser in 10" Dutch oven (Figure 1). Arrange about ⅓ hot coals in cooking ring and set covered Dutch oven on top to preheat for 5 to 10 minutes. Meanwhile, grease 8" round metal baking pan with nonstick cooking spray and spread prepared batter in pan. Set pan on riser in hot Dutch oven. Cover pot and place remaining hot coals on lid. Bake for 12 to 18 minutes or until light golden brown and cooked through. Rotate pot and lid once during cooking and adjust the number of coals on top and bottom as needed for even cooking.

Figure 1: Place four metal nuts, clean pebbles, balls of foil or an inverted metal pie plate in the bottom of the Dutch oven to raise a metal baking pan off the bottom.

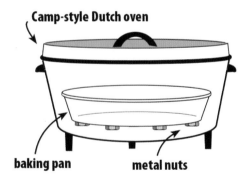

Camp-style Dutch oven

baking pan   metal nuts

MAIN DISHES

In this chapter, cast iron cooks the world, from Hawaiian chicken to Tex-Mex chimichangas, from Chicago-style pizza to the pot pies and pork roasts beloved in the Mid-Atlantic. It's all hearty and yummy, though! If you have a while to cook—say, on a holiday— simmer herb-infused stew in your Dutch oven; or, if speed's your thing, sizzle a steak or Portobello mushroom on your lightly oiled skillet, either over a fire or on your stovetop. Whether you have roasting root vegetables or calzones oozing with cheesy goodness coming up for supper, you'll find that the versatility of cast iron cookware means the possibilities are just about endless!

DEEP-DISH PIZZA

Ingredients
- 1 ¼ tsp. active dry yeast
- 2 tsp. sugar
- 1 tsp. salt
- ¼ tsp. garlic powder
- 1 T. olive oil
- 1 ½ to 2 C. bread flour
- ½ C. prepared pizza sauce
- Toppings such as sliced pepperoni, browned sausage or ground beef, sliced red onion, sliced mushrooms, chopped bell pepper, green or black olives and anchovies
- 1 to 1 ½ C. shredded mozzarella cheese
- 2 T. grated Parmesan cheese
- Freshly ground pepper
- Chopped fresh basil, optional

Preparation
In a medium bowl, combine yeast, sugar and ½ cup very warm water; stir to dissolve and let stand until foamy, about 10 minutes. Stir in salt, garlic powder, oil and just enough flour to make a dough that pulls away from the sides of the bowl. Turn dough out on a lightly floured surface and knead for 5 minutes; cover and let rest 30 to 60 minutes.

On the Stove and in the Oven
Preheat oven to 450°F. Lightly grease skillet with nonstick cooking spray. Roll out dough in circle about 1" larger on all sides than skillet; place dough in pan.* Pinch edges to form rim. Spread sauce over crust. Sprinkle with desired toppings, finishing with mozzarella and Parmesan cheeses. Sprinkle with pepper.

Place skillet on stovetop over high heat for 3 minutes to begin cooking bottom of crust. Transfer skillet to lower rack in oven and bake for 15 to 20 minutes or until crust is golden brown and cheese is melted. Let cool slightly before sliding pizza out of skillet; sprinkle with fresh basil, if desired. Slice to serve. Serve promptly.

For thinner crust, use a 12" skillet and shorten baking time slightly.

12"
with lid

Over the Fire (About 27 hot coals)

Lightly grease a 9" to 10" deep metal pie plate with nonstick cooking spray. Roll out dough in circle about 1" larger on all sides than plate.* Press dough into plate and up sides, pinching edges to form rim. Spread sauce over crust. Sprinkle with desired toppings, finishing with mozzarella and Parmesan cheeses. Sprinkle with pepper. Prepare riser in Dutch oven (see page 95). Set pie plate on riser and cover pot with lid.

Arrange about ⅓ hot coals in cooking ring underneath Dutch oven. Place remaining hot coals on lid. Cook for 15 to 25 minutes or until crust is golden brown and cheese is melted. Rotate pot and lid twice during cooking and adjust the number of coals on top and bottom as needed for even cooking. Let cool slightly before removing pie plate from Dutch oven. Sprinkle with fresh basil, if desired. Slice to serve. Serve promptly.

*For thinner crust, divide dough in half and make two pizzas.
 Shorten cooking time slightly.

RAINY DAY PIZZA CASSEROLE

Let cool 10 to 15 minutes before serving with a salad and garlic toast.

Ingredients

- 3 C. uncooked macaroni, bow tie pasta or spaghetti
- ½ tsp. olive oil
- 2 lb. ground sausage
- 1 C. finely chopped onion
- 1 tsp. minced garlic
- 1 C. sliced fresh mushrooms

- 2 (14 oz.) jars pizza sauce
- 1 (6 oz.) can tomato paste
- 1½ tsp. dried oregano
- 3 C. shredded mozzarella cheese
- ¾ C. grated Parmesan cheese
- 1 (3 oz.) pkg. sliced pepperoni

Preparation

In a large pot of lightly salted boiling water, cook macaroni until tender. (You may use a Dutch oven pot over medium-high heat on stovetop or over a spread of hot coals on a campfire or gas grill.) Drain and toss macaroni with oil; set aside. (This can be done ahead of time, if desired.)

On the Stove and in the Oven

Preheat oven to 350°F. Place Dutch oven on stovetop over medium-high heat and add sausage, onion and garlic. Cook and stir until meat is crumbly and lightly browned and onion is tender; drain. Stir in mushrooms, pizza sauce, tomato paste and oregano; reduce heat to low and simmer sauce mixture for 15 minutes, stirring frequently.

Add cooked pasta and stir to combine. Remove from heat and top with mozzarella and Parmesan cheeses. Arrange pepperoni over top. Place Dutch oven on lower rack in oven and bake uncovered for 25 to 30 minutes or until heated through.

Over the Fire or on the Grill (About 24 hot coals)

Spread hot coals in flat layer underneath Dutch oven. Combine sausage, onion and garlic in pot. Cook and stir until meat is crumbly and lightly browned and onion is tender; drain. Stir in mushrooms, pizza sauce, tomato paste and oregano.

To reduce heat, push about ⅔ coals to one side of Dutch oven and simmer the sauce mixture over remaining coals for 15 minutes, stirring frequently. Stir in cooked pasta until well combined. Top with mozzarella and Parmesan cheeses; arrange pepperoni over top. Cover pot with lid.

Rearrange hot coals under Dutch oven to make cooking ring and place remaining hot coals on lid. Cook for 20 to 30 minutes or until heated through. Rotate pot and lid twice during cooking and adjust the number of coals on top and bottom as needed for even cooking.

PEPPERONI ROLL-UPS

PIE IRON RECIPE

Ingredients

> Refrigerated crescent dough sheet
> Sun-dried tomato pesto
> Pepperoni
> Mozzarella cheese

Directions

Grease your pie iron heavily with cooking spray. Unroll the dough and spread with as much pesto as you please. Toss on pepperoni and cheese; roll it up nice and tight. Pinch the edges so the filling doesn't escape. Cut the roll into 12 slices (snails). Lay several snails in the iron. Close the iron and hold over nice warm coals until browned and beautiful on both sides.

FIRESIDE LASAGNA

Ingredients

- 1½ lbs. lean ground beef
- ½ C. diced onion
- 1 (24 oz.) jar spaghetti sauce
- 3 eggs
- 2 C. shredded mozzarella cheese, divided
- ¼ C. grated Parmesan cheese
- 2 C. cottage cheese
- 1½ tsp. dried oregano
- 1 tsp. garlic powder
- 14 uncooked lasagna noodles
- ¾ C. hot water

Preparation

In a bowl, mix eggs, 1¾ cups mozzarella cheese, Parmesan and cottage cheeses, oregano and garlic powder.

On the Stove and in the Oven

Preheat oven to 325°F. Meanwhile, place Dutch oven on stovetop over medium heat and cook beef and onion until meat is crumbly and onion is tender. Transfer to a bowl and stir in sauce.

Break 5 noodles to cover bottom of pot. Top with the following layers: ⅓ of the meat mixture, half the cheese mixture, 5 noodles, half the remaining meat mixture, all remaining cheese mixture, last 4 noodles and rest of meat.

Pour hot water around inside edge of pot and transfer to center rack in oven to cook uncovered for 45 minutes or until noodles are tender. Remove from heat and let rest for 10 minutes. Before serving, sprinkle with remaining ¼ cup mozzarella and let melt.

Over the Fire (About 24 hot coals)

Spread about 24 hot coals in a flat layer under Dutch oven. Cook beef and onion until meat is crumbly and onion is tender. Transfer to a bowl and stir in sauce.

Break 5 noodles to cover bottom of pot. Top with the following layers: ⅓ of the meat mixture, half the cheese mixture, 5 noodles, half the remaining meat mixture, all remaining cheese mixture, last 4 noodles and rest of meat. Pour hot water around inside edge of pot and cover with lid.

Rearrange 12 of the hot coals in a ring under the Dutch oven and place the rest on lid. Cook 45 minutes or until noodles are tender, rotating pot and lid several times and replenishing coals to maintain temperature. Remove from heat and let rest uncovered for 10 minutes. Before serving, sprinkle with remaining ¼ cup mozzarella and let melt.

MAMA'S CHICKEN POT PIE

Serve in bowls, crust side up.

Ingredients

- 1 (9") refrigerated pie crust
- 1 C. sliced carrot coins
- ½ C. chopped onion
- 2 tsp. minced garlic
- 1 (4 oz.) can sliced mushrooms, drained
- 1 C. frozen corn, partially thawed
- 1 C. frozen shredded hash browns, partially thawed
- ½ C. frozen peas, partially thawed
- 2 T. olive oil
- Salt and pepper to taste
- ½ tsp. poultry seasoning, optional
- 3 C. chopped cooked chicken*
- 1 (10.7 oz.) can cream of potato soup
- 1 (10.7 oz.) can cream of chicken soup
- ⅔ C. fat-free half-and-half

Preparation

Let pie crust stand at room temperature for 15 minutes (in wrapper). In a medium bowl, combine carrots, onion and garlic; in another bowl, combine mushrooms, corn, hash browns and peas.

On the Stove and in the Oven

Preheat oven to 375°F. Meanwhile, place skillet on stovetop over medium heat and add oil. When hot, add carrots and onion; sauté until crisp-tender. Stir in garlic and sauté briefly. Add mushrooms, corn, hash browns and peas, tossing to blend. Season with salt, pepper and poultry seasoning as desired. Cook about 2 minutes or until heated through, stirring frequently. Stir in chicken, both soups and half-and-half; mix gently to blend. Cook until warmed.

Remove skillet from heat. Unroll crust and place over chicken filling to cover, crimping edges as needed. Cut several slits in crust to vent steam. Place skillet on center rack in oven and bake for 40 to 45 minutes or until crust is golden brown and filling is bubbly. Let stand several minutes before serving.

Variation: In place of chicken, you may use leftover cooked turkey or, for convenience, try rotisserie or canned chunk chicken.

10"
with lid

Over the Fire (24+ hot coals)

Spread hot coals in flat layer underneath Dutch oven. Add oil. When hot, sauté carrots and onion until crisp-tender. Stir in garlic and sauté briefly. Add mushrooms, corn, hash browns and peas, tossing to blend. Season with salt, pepper and poultry seasoning as desired. Cook about 2 minutes or until heated through, stirring frequently. Stir in chicken, both soups and half-and-half; mix gently to blend. Cook until warmed.

Remove Dutch oven from heat. Unroll crust and place over chicken filling to cover, crimping edges as needed. Cut several slits in crust to vent steam. Cover pot with lid. Rearrange about ⅓ hot coals to make cooking ring underneath Dutch oven; place remaining hot coals on lid. Cook for 40 to 50 minutes or until crust is golden brown and filling is bubbly. Rotate pot and lid several times during cooking and replenish coals on lid toward end of cooking time to promote browning. Let stand several minutes before serving.

PIE IRON POT PIE

PIE IRON
RECIPE

Ingredients
› Refrigerated pie crust
› Chopped onions
› Cooked chicken
› Canned mixed veggies, drained
› Salt & pepper
› Cream of chicken soup

Directions

Grease a pie iron and cut pie crust to fit. Line one side of iron with crust. Add onions, chicken, veggies, salt, pepper and a few spoonsful of soup. Add another pie crust on top, pressing edges together. Close the iron and cook in hot coals, adding a few coals on top if you want to speed things along. When it's golden and flaky, it's done.

DUTCH OVEN ROASTED
CHICKEN & VEGETABLES

Serve with a large slotted spoon, drizzling juices over chicken and vegetables as desired.

Ingredients

- 1 (4 to 5 lb.) whole chicken, cut into pieces
- ⅓ C. flour
- 1 T. Montreal Chicken Seasoning or chicken rub*
- 1 onion
- 3 large carrots, peeled
- 2 potatoes, peeled
- ½ butternut squash, peeled
- 1 zucchini
- 1 red bell pepper, cored, seeded
- 2 T. olive oil
- 2 C. fresh mushrooms
- Salt and pepper to taste
- 2 sprigs fresh rosemary (or 2 tsp. dried)

Preparation

Cut off excess fat from chicken; remove skin, if desired. In a shallow bowl, mix flour and Montreal Chicken Seasoning. Coat all sides of chicken pieces in flour mixture; set aside. Cut onion, carrots, potatoes and squash into large chunks. Slice zucchini and bell pepper.

In the Oven

Preheat oven to 350°F. Meanwhile, place Dutch oven on stovetop over medium-high heat and add oil. When hot, brown chicken pieces on both sides. Remove pot from heat; tuck onion pieces underneath chicken. Arrange carrots, potatoes, zucchini, squash and mushrooms around chicken. Season with salt and pepper; top with rosemary.

Cover Dutch oven and place on lower rack in oven. Cook about 1 hour or until chicken and vegetables are tender. Add bell pepper during last 15 minutes of cooking time. Let stand several minutes before serving.

Chicken Rub

In a small bowl, stir together ½ teaspoon each of curry powder, dried sage, dried rosemary, dried coriander, dried thyme and ¼ teaspoon garlic powder.

12"
with lid

Over the Fire (24+ hot coals)

Spread hot coals in flat layer underneath Dutch oven. Heat oil and brown chicken pieces on both sides. Tuck onion pieces underneath chicken. Arrange carrots, potatoes, zucchini, squash and mushrooms around chicken. Season with salt and pepper; top with rosemary. Cover pot with lid.

Rearrange about ⅓ hot coals to make cooking ring underneath Dutch oven; place remaining hot coals on lid. Cook for 50 to 60 minutes or until chicken and vegetables are tender. Add bell pepper during last 15 minutes of cooking time. Rotate pot and lid several times during cooking and replenish coals on top and bottom as needed to maintain cooking temperature. Let stand several minutes before serving.

FAMILY-STYLE
CHICKEN & RICE

Serve family style with a large spoon.

Ingredients

- 1 (10.75 oz.) can cream of chicken soup
- 1 (10.75 oz.) can cream of mushroom soup
- 1 C. sour cream
- 2 C. uncooked white rice
- ¾ C. chopped onion
- 6 fresh mushrooms, sliced
- 2 large carrots, peeled and sliced
- 1 T. Worcestershire sauce
- 1 to 2 tsp. garlic powder
- ½ tsp. salt
- ½ tsp. white pepper
- 1 tsp. paprika
- 5 or 6 bone-in chicken breasts

Preparation

In a large bowl, combine both cans of soup, sour cream and 2 cups water; whisk until well blended. Stir in rice, onion, mushrooms, carrots, Worcestershire sauce and garlic powder; set aside. In a small bowl, mix salt, pepper and paprika; sprinkle evenly over chicken pieces.

Variation: To use a 12" Dutch oven, cook just five chicken breasts and reduce the number of hot coals to 24.

In the Oven

Preheat oven to 325°F. Lightly grease bottom of Dutch oven with vegetable oil. Transfer prepared rice mixture into pot and spread evenly; arrange chicken on top of rice. Cover Dutch oven and place on center rack in oven. Cook 1 ¼ to 1 ½ hours or until chicken is cooked through and rice and vegetables are tender. Let stand several minutes before serving.

Over the Fire (28+ hot coals)

Lightly grease bottom of Dutch oven* with vegetable oil. Transfer prepared rice mixture into pot and spread evenly; arrange chicken on top of rice. Cover Dutch oven with lid.

Arrange about ⅓ hot coals in cooking ring underneath Dutch oven; place remaining hot coals on lid. Cook about 1½ hours or until chicken is cooked through and rice and vegetables are tender. Rotate pot and lid several times during cooking and replenish coals on top and bottom as needed to maintain cooking temperature.

BBQ CHEESY CHICKEN SANDWICH

Ingredients

- White bread
- Cheddar cheese
- Cooked chicken
- Red onion slices
- BBQ sauce
- Smoked Gouda cheese

Directions

Coat pie iron with cooking spray. Set one slice of bread in iron. Add cheddar, chicken, onion rings, BBQ sauce and Gouda. Set another bread slice on top. Close the iron and heat over hot coals until bread is crisp and toasty.

HAWAIIAN-STYLE CHICKEN

Ingredients

- 1 C. peach preserves
- ½ C. barbecue sauce
- 2 T. soy sauce
- ½ C. diced onion
- 1 green bell pepper, cored, seeded
- ⅓ C. flour
- ½ tsp. paprika
- ½ tsp. salt
- Dash of pepper
- 4 boneless, skinless chicken breast halves
- 2 T. vegetable oil
- 1 (8 oz.) can sliced water chestnuts, drained
- Hot cooked rice

Preparation

In a medium bowl, stir together peach preserves, barbecue sauce, soy sauce and onion; reserve sauce for later use. Slice bell pepper into strips. In a shallow bowl, combine flour, paprika, salt and pepper; mix well. Coat both sides of chicken breast halves in flour mixture.

On the Stove and in the Oven

Preheat oven to 350°F. Meanwhile, place skillet on stovetop over medium-high heat and add oil. When hot, brown chicken pieces on each side for 3 minutes. Remove skillet from heat and pour off excess oil. Pour reserved barbecue sauce mixture over chicken.

Cover skillet and place on center rack in oven to cook for 35 minutes. Remove lid and stir in bell pepper and water chestnuts. Cover and return to oven to cook about 15 minutes more or until tender. Serve with cooked rice.

Over the Fire (26+ hot coals)

Spread hot coals in flat layer underneath Dutch oven. Pour oil into pot. When hot, brown chicken pieces on each side for 3 minutes. Remove pot from coals and pour off excess oil. Pour reserved barbeque sauce mixture over chicken and cover pot with lid.

Rearrange about ⅓ hot coals to make cooking ring underneath Dutch oven; place remaining hot coals on lid. Cook for 30 to 40 minutes, rotating pot and lid twice during cooking and replenishing coals on top and bottom as needed to maintain cooking temperature. Remove lid and stir in bell pepper and water chestnuts. Cover and cook about 15 minutes more or until tender. Serve with cooked rice.

> **Alternate Cooking Method:** Use a kitchen-style Dutch oven with lid and cook on a grate over medium heat (hot coals or grill).

HAWAIIAN BBQ QUESADILLAS

Ingredients

- Flour tortillas
- Monterey Jack cheese
- Cooked ham
- Cooked bacon
- Crushed pineapple, drained
- BBQ sauce
- Pickled banana peppers, drained
- Fresh cilantro

Directions

Grease a pie iron. Cut tortillas into pieces a little bigger than the iron and set one piece inside. Add cheese, ham and bacon. Finish it off with pineapple, BBQ sauce, peppers and cilantro. Add another tortilla piece. Close iron, trim off excess and cook over hot coals until hot and toasted. Serve with BBQ sauce.

FANCY BEANS & FRANKS

Ingredients

- 2 bacon strips
- 1 (1 lb.) pkg. hot dogs
- 1 T. lemon juice
- 1 T. Worcestershire sauce
- 1 T. brown sugar
- 1 tsp. salt
- ½ tsp. chili powder
- ¼ C. ketchup
- ⅛ tsp. garlic salt
- ¼ C. chopped onion
- 1 (8 oz.) can tomato sauce
- ¼ C. flour
- 1 (16 oz.) can kidney beans, undrained

Preparation

Chop bacon into small pieces. Slice hot dogs into 1" pieces. In a small bowl, stir together lemon juice, Worcestershire sauce, brown sugar, salt, chili powder, ketchup and garlic salt; set aside.

On the Stove

Place Dutch oven on stovetop over medium-high heat and add bacon; fry until crisp. Remove bacon pieces to drain on paper towels; reserve for later use. Add onion to bacon grease in pot and sauté until light brown. Reduce heat to medium-low and stir in tomato sauce and flour; cook until slightly thickened, stirring constantly.

Add beans and stir to combine. Stir in prepared lemon juice mixture. When bubbly, cover with lid and simmer for 15 minutes. Add hot dog pieces, stirring to coat, and simmer for 10 minutes more. Just before serving, sprinkle with reserved bacon pieces. Serve warm as a main or side dish.

Over the Fire (About 15 coals)

Spread the hot coals in a flat layer underneath Dutch oven. Place bacon in pot and cook until crisp. Remove bacon pieces to drain on paper towels; reserve for later use. Add onion to bacon grease in pot and sauté until light brown. Stir in tomato sauce and flour; cook until slightly thickened, stirring constantly. Add beans and stir to combine. Stir in prepared lemon juice mixture. When bubbly, cover with lid and remove pot from heat.

Rearrange about ⅓ hot coals to make cooking ring underneath Dutch oven; transfer remaining hot coals to lid. Bring mixture to simmer and cook for 15 minutes. Remove lid and stir in hot dog pieces. Cover and cook for 10 minutes more or until heated through. Rotate pot and lid once during cooking and adjust the number of coals on top and bottom as needed for even cooking. Serve warm as a main or side dish.

BEEF & BEAN CHIMICHANGAS

Serve with lettuce, tomatoes, corn, cheese and black olives.

Ingredients

- Corn tortillas
- Refried beans
- Whole kernel corn, drained
- Salsa
- Cooked taco meat
- Mexican cheese

Directions

Set a tortilla in a greased pie iron. Spread with refried beans and add some corn. Now add salsa, taco meat and cheese. Top with another tortilla and close the iron. Cut off excess tortilla and place in hot coals until both sides are toasted.

CRUNCHY POTATOES & HAM

Serve promptly. Add a side salad or raw vegetables and dip to complete the meal.

Ingredients

- 1½ C. diced ham
- 3 C. diced raw potatoes
- ¼ C. butter
- 1 C. chopped onion
- 3 T. flour
- 2 C. milk

- 1 T. parsley flakes
- 1 tsp. dried minced garlic
- Salt and pepper to taste
- ½ C. shredded cheddar cheese
- 3 T. Italian breadcrumbs

Preparation

In a medium bowl, combine ham and potatoes.

On the Stove and in the Oven

Preheat oven to 400°F. Meanwhile, place Dutch oven on stovetop over medium heat and melt butter. Add onion and sauté until tender. Stir in flour until bubbly and light brown. Gradually whisk in milk and cook until thickened. Stir in parsley and garlic.

Remove pot from heat and add ham and potato mixture to sauce, stirring gently to coat. Season with salt and pepper. Spread mixture in pot and sprinkle with cheese and bread crumbs. Place pot on center rack in oven and bake uncovered for 20 minutes or until heated through and lightly browned.

Over the Fire (26 hot coals)

Spread ½ hot coals in flat layer underneath Dutch oven. Melt butter; add onion and sauté until tender. Stir in flour until bubbly and light brown. Gradually whisk in milk and cook until thickened. Stir in parsley and garlic.

Remove pot from heat and add ham and potato mixture to sauce, stirring gently to coat. Season with salt and pepper. Spread mixture evenly in pot and sprinkle with cheese and bread crumbs. Cover pot with lid.

Rearrange hot coals to make cooking ring that just fits underneath Dutch oven; place remaining hot coals on lid. Cook about 20 minutes or until heated through and lightly browned. Rotate pot and lid halfway through cooking time and adjust the number of coals on top and bottom as needed for even cooking.

CHEESY SPINACH CALZONES

Serve with pizza sauce.

Ingredients

- Refrigerated pizza dough
- Frozen spinach, thawed & drained
- Onions, bell peppers & mushrooms
- Minced garlic
- Alfredo sauce
- Mozzarella cheese
- Salt & pepper

Directions

Coat a pie iron with cooking spray. Roll dough thin and cut into pieces to fit iron; press one piece inside. Pile on the spinach, chopped onions and sliced peppers. Add sliced mushrooms, garlic, Alfredo sauce and cheese; sprinkle with salt and pepper. Add another dough piece, close the iron and cook over warm coals. Turn occasionally until dough is cooked and nicely browned.

OLD-FASHIONED PORK ROAST

Serve with mashed potatoes and gravy.

Ingredients

- 1 (2 to 3 lb.) boneless pork loin roast
- 1 tsp. salt
- 2 tsp. pepper
- 1 tsp. seasoned salt
- 1 onion
- 1 T. olive oil
- 2½ tsp. minced garlic
- 1 T. Kitchen Bouquet Browning & Seasoning Sauce
- 2 T. cornstarch

Preparation

Cut off excess fat from roast. Season all sides of pork with salt, pepper and seasoned salt. Thinly slice onion.

On the Stove and in the Oven

Preheat oven to 350°F. Meanwhile, place Dutch oven on stovetop over medium-high heat and add oil. When hot, brown roast on all sides. Add onion and garlic; sauté until tender. Mix Kitchen Bouquet with 2 cups water; pour water mixture into Dutch oven and bring to a boil. Cover pot and remove from heat.

Place Dutch oven on lower rack in oven. Cook for 1 hour or until a meat thermometer reaches 145°F, turning roast after 30 minutes. Remove roast to a platter and tent with foil to keep warm. Let meat stand 15 minutes before slicing.

To make gravy, set Dutch oven on stovetop over medium-high heat. In a small bowl, mix ½ cup cold water and cornstarch. Whisk cornstarch mixture into drippings in pot; boil and stir until thickened.

Over the Fire (22+ hot coals)

Spread hot coals in flat layer underneath Dutch oven. Heat oil and brown roast on all sides. Add onion and garlic; sauté until tender. Mix Kitchen Bouquet with 2 cups water. Pour water mixture into Dutch oven and bring to a boil. Cover pot with lid.

Rearrange about ½ hot coals to make cooking ring underneath Dutch oven; place remaining hot coals on lid. Cook about 1 hour or until a meat thermometer reaches 145°F, turning roast after 30 minutes. Rotate pot and lid several times during cooking and replenish coals on top and bottom as needed to maintain cooking temperature. Remove roast to a platter and tent with foil to keep warm. Let meat stand 15 minutes before slicing.

To make gravy, transfer several coals from lid to cooking ring underneath Dutch oven and follow On the Stove and in the Oven directions above.

TOASTY BLT

Ingredients

- Whole wheat bread
- Mayo
- Tomatoes
- Cooked bacon
- Lettuce leaves

Directions

Grease a pie iron and put a bread slice inside; smear with a little mayo. Slice tomatoes and add a couple slices to the bread. Add bacon before covering with another bread slice. Squeeze the iron shut, trim bread and hold in hot coals until toasted on both sides.

CAST IRON PORK CHOP BAKE

Ingredients
- ¼ C. lite soy sauce
- 3 T. honey
- 1 tsp. chili powder
- 1 tsp. curry powder
- Pepper to taste
- 5 bacon strips

- 4 pork chops (1" thick)
- ⅔ C. chopped onion
- ½ tsp. minced garlic
- Hot cooked brown rice or noodles

Preparation
In a small bowl, combine soy sauce, honey, chili powder, curry powder and pepper; mix well and reserve for later use. Cut bacon into small pieces.

On the Stove and in the Oven

Preheat oven to 350°F. Meanwhile, place skillet on stovetop over medium heat and brown pork chops for 5 to 6 minutes on each side. Remove chops to a platter and tent with foil to keep warm. Pour off any accumulated grease.

Lightly brown bacon in skillet; then add onion and sauté over medium heat for 5 minutes. Add garlic and sauté briefly. Pour off excess grease and stir in reserved soy sauce mixture. Place pork chops back in skillet and turn to coat with sauce. Cover skillet and place on center rack in oven to bake for 20 to 25 minutes or until chops are cooked through and tender. Let cooked chops stand at least 3 minutes before serving. Serve with cooked rice or noodles.

Over the Fire (About 26 hot coals)

Spread hot coals in flat layer underneath Dutch oven. Add pork chops and brown meat for 5 to 6 minutes on each side. Remove chops to a platter and tent with foil to keep warm. Pour off any accumulated grease.

Lightly brown bacon in Dutch oven; then add onion and sauté for 5 minutes. Add garlic and sauté briefly. Pour off excess grease and stir in reserved soy sauce mixture.

Rearrange about ⅓ hot coals to make cooking ring underneath Dutch oven. Place pork chops back in pot and turn to coat with sauce. Cover Dutch oven and place remaining hot coals on lid. Cook for 20 to 30 minutes or until chops are cooked through and tender. Rotate pot and lid twice during cooking time and adjust the number of coals on top and bottom as needed for even cooking. Let cooked chops stand at least 3 minutes before serving. Serve with cooked rice or noodles.

PESTO PANINI

Ingredients

- Butter
- Italian bread
- Your favorite pesto
- Fire-roasted tomatoes, drained
- Sliced salami
- Mozzarella cheese

Directions

Butter bread slices and lay the buttered sides in the iron. Fill one side with pesto, tomatoes, salami and cheese. Close it up and trim off bread; place in warm coals. Flip occasionally while cooking.

HAWAIIAN-STYLE KIELBASA

Ingredients

- 2 T. butter
- 1 ¼ C. water
- 1 (14 oz.) pkg. kielbasa sausage, sliced
- 1 red bell pepper, coarsely chopped
- 1 green bell pepper, coarsely chopped
- 1 (8 oz.) can pineapple chunks
- 1 (6.2 oz.) pkg. fast-cook long grain and wild rice mix with seasoning packet
- ½ C. pineapple preserves

On the Stove and in the Oven

Preheat oven to 325°F. Meanwhile, place Dutch oven on stovetop over medium heat. Combine butter and water in the pot and bring to a boil. Add the sausage, bell peppers, pineapple, rice, seasoning from packet and pineapple preserves. Stir well and transfer Dutch oven to center rack in oven to cook uncovered for 40 to 45 minutes, stirring twice. Remove from heat and let rest for 10 minutes before serving.

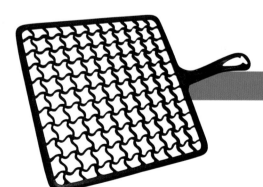

VINTAGE SPOTLIGHT

"Duck Bill" Broiler, circa 1800. This piece was used on the fireplace hearth.

12"
with lid

Over the Fire (About 24 hot coals)

Spread about 24 hot coals in a flat layer under the Dutch oven. Combine butter and water in the pot and bring to a boil. Add the sausage, bell peppers, pineapple, rice, seasoning from packet and pineapple preserves. Stir well and cover pot with lid.

Rearrange 10 of the hot coals in a ring under the Dutch oven and move the remaining coals to the lid. Cook 40 to 45 minutes, rotating pot and lid every 15 minutes and stirring twice; let coals burn down before replenishing. Remove from heat and let rest for 10 minutes before serving.

CHUCK WAGON BEEF STEW

Serve steaming hot in bowls, garnished with Parmesan cheese and basil, if desired.

Ingredients

> 3 potatoes
> 2 parsnips
> ½ (16 oz.) pkg. baby carrots
> 1 C. frozen corn or mixed vegetables
> 2 T. flour
> 1 tsp. paprika
> 1½ tsp. chili powder, divided
> 1 tsp. salt
> 1 lb. cubed beef stew meat

> 3 T. olive oil
> 1 C. chopped onion
> ½ tsp. minced garlic
> 3 C. beef broth or bouillon
> ½ tsp. red pepper flakes
> Seasoned salt and pepper to taste
> Shaved Parmesan cheese, optional
> Fresh basil leaves, optional

Preparation

Scrub and cube potatoes. Peel and slice parsnips. Place potatoes, parsnips, carrots and corn in a large bowl; reserve for later use. In a gallon-size resealable plastic bag, combine flour, paprika, 1 teaspoon chili powder and salt. Add beef and shake to coat cubes well.

On the Stove and in the Oven

Preheat oven to 275°F. Meanwhile, place skillet on stovetop over medium-high heat and add oil. When hot, brown meat on all sides. Add onion; sauté until tender. Stir in garlic and sauté briefly. Reduce heat to medium-low and stir in broth, red pepper flakes, remaining ½ teaspoon chili powder and reserved vegetables. Sprinkle with seasoned salt and pepper. Cover skillet and transfer to oven. Cook about 3 hours or until meat is very tender.

Variation

Use a kitchen-style Dutch oven with lid on a grate over medium heat (hot coals or gas grill), simmering until tender. Adjust cooking time as needed.

Alternate Cooking Method

Add chopped tomatoes and mushrooms to stew.

Over the Fire (16+ hot coals)

Spread hot coals in flat layer underneath Dutch oven and add oil. When hot, brown meat on all sides. Add onion; sauté until tender. Stir in garlic and sauté briefly. Stir in broth, red pepper flakes, remaining ½ teaspoon chili powder and reserved vegetables. Sprinkle with seasoned salt and pepper. Cover pot with lid.

Rearrange about ½ hot coals to make cooking ring underneath Dutch oven; place remaining hot coals on lid. Simmer slowly for 2 to 3 hours, rotating pot and lid several times every hour and replenishing coals on top and bottom as needed to maintain cooking temperature. If necessary, add water to keep liquid at a low simmer.

SIMMERING CIDER
BEEF STEW

SERVES 8-10

Ingredients

- ⅓ C. flour
- 1½ tsp. paprika
- Salt and black pepper to taste
- 2 lbs. beef stew meat
- 3 T. vegetable oil
- 2 C. hot water
- 1 T. beef bouillon granules
- 1½ C. apple cider
- ¼ C. ketchup
- 1 tsp. minced garlic
- 2 C. chopped cabbage
- 4 parsnips, peeled and chopped
- 1 onion, diced
- 2 C. baby carrots
- 4 potatoes, peeled and cubed
- 2 C. frozen green beans
- 1 (8.75 oz.) can whole kernel corn, drained
- 2 T. Worcestershire sauce

Preparation

Mix the flour, paprika, salt and pepper in a large zippered bag. Add meat cubes; seal bag and shake well to coat.

12" with lid

On the Stove

Place Dutch oven on stovetop over medium heat. Heat oil and brown the meat on all sides. Stir in water, bouillon, cider, ketchup and garlic. Cover pot with lid and simmer until meat is tender, about 2 hours.

Add cabbage, parsnips, onion, carrots, potatoes, green beans, corn and Worcestershire sauce. Cover and simmer until vegetables are tender, about 1 hour.

12" with lid

Over the Fire (About 24 hot coals)

Spread about 24 hot coals in a flat layer under the Dutch oven. Heat oil and brown the meat on all sides. Stir in water, bouillon, cider, ketchup and garlic. Cover pot with lid.

Rearrange 12 of the hot coals in a ring under the Dutch oven and move remaining coals to the lid. Simmer until meat is tender, about 2 hours. Rotate pot and lid several times every hour and replenish coals as needed for simmering.

Add cabbage, parsnips, onion, carrots, potatoes, green beans, corn and Worcestershire sauce. Cover and simmer with coals on top and bottom until vegetables are tender, about 1 hour. Rotate pot and replenish coals when necessary.

This dish is a great way to stay warm on a cool fall night.

CALICO CHILI

Serve in bowls garnished with a few corn chips and cheese, if desired.
Bake cornbread, biscuits, or sourdough bread to serve with chili.

Ingredients

- 2 bell peppers (assortment of green, yellow, red, orange), cored, seeded
- 1 lb. lean ground beef
- ¾ C. chopped onion
- 1 tsp. minced garlic
- 1 (16 oz.) can chili beans, undrained
- 1 (16 oz.) can Northern beans, drained, rinsed
- 1 (14.5 oz.) can diced tomatoes, undrained
- 1¼ C. tomato juice or V-8
- 1⅓ C. frozen or canned whole kernel corn, drained
- 1 (1 oz.) env. ranch salad dressing mix
- Corn chips, optional
- Shredded cheddar cheese, optional

Preparation

Chop bell peppers to measure 1¾ cups.

On the Stove

Place Dutch oven on stovetop over medium-high heat and add ground beef and onion. Cook and stir until meat is crumbly and lightly browned and onion is tender; drain.

Add garlic and bell peppers; cook for 3 minutes to soften. Stir in 1 cup water, chili beans, Northern beans, tomatoes, tomato juice, corn and dressing mix until well combined. Bring to a simmer, stirring frequently. Reduce heat to low, cover and simmer slowly for 20 to 30 minutes, stirring occasionally, until flavors are blended.

Over the Fire or on the Grill (24 hot coals)

Spread hot coals in flat layer underneath Dutch oven. Add ground beef and onion to pot. Cook and stir until meat is crumbly and lightly browned and onion is tender; drain. Add garlic and bell peppers; cook for 3 minutes to soften. Stir in 1 cup water, chili beans, Northern beans, tomatoes, tomato juice, corn and dressing mix until well combined. Bring to a simmer, stirring frequently. Cover pot with lid.

Rearrange about ½ hot coals to make cooking ring underneath Dutch oven; place remaining hot coals on lid. Simmer slowly for 20 to 30 minutes, stirring occasionally, until flavors are blended. Rotate pot and lid once during cooking time and adjust the number of coals on top and bottom as needed for even cooking.

FIRESIDE SLOPPY JOES

PIE IRON RECIPE

Ingredients

- Potato bread
- 1 can of sloppy joe mix
- 1 lb. cooked ground beef
- American or Swiss cheese

Directions

Coat a pie iron with cooking spray and set a slice of bread inside. Stir together sloppy joe mix and ground beef; spoon some onto the bread. Add cheese. Top with another slice of bread, close the iron and trim off the excess. Hold above hot coals until the filling is hot. The meat gets sealed inside the bread, making for easy eating.

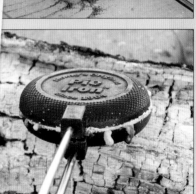

HEARTY BEEF GOULASH

Serve when cheese is thoroughly melted.

Ingredients

> 1 yellow onion
> 1 green bell pepper
> 2 T. olive oil
> 1 lb. lean ground beef
> 1 C. sliced fresh mushrooms
> 1 tsp. minced garlic
> 1 C. frozen corn, partially thawed

> 2 (10.75 oz.) cans tomato soup
> ¼ tsp. paprika
> ½ tsp. cayenne pepper
> 2 tsp. salt
> 1 tsp. pepper
> 1 (12 oz.) pkg. pasta shells
> 3 C. shredded cheddar cheese

Preparation

Dice onion and bell pepper.

★ ★ ★ ★ DUTCH OVEN DETAILS ★ ★ ★ ★

Soupy Situation

After cooking soups, stews and other foods with a high water content, you may need to reseason your cookware.

On the Stove and in the Oven

Preheat oven to 350°F. Meanwhile, place Dutch oven on stovetop over medium-high heat and add oil. When hot, brown ground beef. Add onion, bell pepper, mushrooms and garlic; sauté until peppers are tender. Stir in corn, both cans of soup, 2½ soup cans hot water, paprika, cayenne pepper, salt and pepper. Bring mixture to a boil and then stir in pasta shells. Cover with lid and place Dutch oven on center rack in oven to cook for 40 minutes.

Remove lid, sprinkle cheese over pasta mixture and bake uncovered for 15 minutes more or until cheese is melted.

Over the Fire (26+ hot coals)

Spread hot coals in flat layer underneath Dutch oven and add oil. When hot, brown ground beef. Add onion, bell pepper, mushrooms and garlic; sauté until peppers are tender. Stir in corn, both cans of soup, 2½ soup cans hot water, paprika, cayenne pepper, salt and pepper. Bring mixture to a boil and then stir in pasta shells. Cover with lid.

Rearrange about ⅓ hot coals to make cooking ring underneath Dutch oven; place remaining hot coals on lid. Cook about 45 minutes or until heated through. Rotate pot and lid several times during cooking and replenish coals on top and bottom as needed to maintain cooking temperature.

Remove lid and sprinkle cheese over pasta mixture; cover and cook about 15 minutes more or until cheese is melted.

VINTAGE SPOTLIGHT

Gem Pans by Wagner Manufacturing Company, circa 1915. These pans were used to make corn bread and other baked treats.

SPICY CHILI MAC

Ingredients

- 1 lb. ground beef
- 1 onion, chopped
- 2 (10 oz.) cans mild diced tomatoes with green chilies
- 1 C. water
- 1½ C. uncooked rotini pasta or elbow macaroni
- Seasoned salt and black pepper to taste
- ½ C. shredded cheddar cheese

On the Stove

Place Dutch oven on stovetop over medium heat. Cook the beef and onion until meat is brown and crumbly and onion is tender. Stir in tomatoes with chilies, water and pasta; sprinkle with seasoned salt and pepper as desired.

Bring mixture to a boil and cover pot with lid. Let simmer about 20 minutes or until pasta is tender. Stir after 15 minutes. Dish it up hot and sprinkle with cheese.

Over the Fire (20 hot coals)

Spread about 20 hot coals in a flat layer under the Dutch oven. Cook the beef and onion until meat is brown and crumbly and onion is tender. Stir in tomatoes with chilies, water and pasta; sprinkle with seasoned salt and pepper as desired. Bring mixture to a boil and cover pot with lid.

Rearrange 7 of the hot coals in a ring under the Dutch oven and move remaining coals to the lid. Let simmer about 20 minutes or until pasta is tender. Stir after 15 minutes and then rotate pot and lid to finish cooking. Dish it up hot and sprinkle with cheese.

Tip: When you begin to smell the food inside your Dutch oven, it's a sign the dish is almost ready to eat!

DUTCH OVEN MEATLOAF

Serve slices of hot meatloaf with baked or mashed potatoes.

Ingredients

- 1 onion
- 4 lb. lean ground beef
- 2 C. bread crumbs
- 3 eggs, lightly beaten
- 1 C. milk
- 1 C. ketchup, divided
- 2 tsp. salt
- ½ tsp. pepper
- Garlic powder to taste
- Vegetable oil

Preparation

Finely chop onion and place in a large bowl. Add ground beef, breadcrumbs, eggs, milk, ½ cup ketchup, salt, pepper and garlic powder as desired. Mix thoroughly.

In the Oven

Preheat oven to 350°F. Lightly grease bottom of Dutch oven with oil. Spread prepared meatloaf mixture in pot; cover with lid. Place on lower rack in oven and cook for 50 to 60 minutes.

Uncover and spread remaining ½ cup ketchup over meatloaf. Return to oven to bake uncovered for 15 minutes more or until fully cooked (160°F internal temperature). Let stand a few minutes before slicing.

Over the Fire (24+ hot coals)

Lightly grease bottom of Dutch oven with vegetable oil. Spread prepared meatloaf mixture in pot and cover with lid.

Arrange about ½ hot coals in cooking ring underneath Dutch oven. Place remaining hot coals on lid. Cook about 40 minutes, rotating pot and lid several times during cooking and replenishing coals on top and bottom as needed to maintain temperature.

Transfer a few hot coals from bottom ring to lid and continue to cook about 20 minutes more. Carefully remove lid and spread remaining ½ cup ketchup over meatloaf; cover again and cook for 15 minutes more or until fully cooked (160°F internal temperature). Let stand a few minutes before slicing.

If you're worried bare cast iron might not impress at your next dinner party, break out your enamel pieces for some colorful additions to the dining table.

SIMPLE ROUND STEAK

Ingredients

- 1½ to 2 lb. round steak
- 1 onion
- 1 green bell pepper, cored, seeded
- 1 (12 oz.) can cola
- ¾ C. ketchup
- 2 T. olive oil
- Salt and pepper to taste
- Hot cooked noodles

Preparation

Cut round steak into eight equal strips. Slice onion and bell pepper. In a medium bowl, whisk together cola and ketchup.

On the Stove and in the Oven

Preheat oven to 325°F. Meanwhile, place skillet on stovetop over medium heat and add oil. When hot, brown steak pieces on both sides. Add onion and sauté until tender. Remove pan from heat and remove meat and onion from skillet; pour off oil.

Return meat and onion to skillet and add bell pepper. Pour prepared cola mixture over meat; season with salt and pepper as desired. Cover with lid and place skillet on center rack in oven to cook about 1 hour or until meat is tender and sauce thickens. Serve with sauce and cooked noodles.

Over the Fire (24+ hot coals)

Spread hot coals in flat layer underneath Dutch oven and add oil. When hot, brown steak pieces on both sides. Add onion and sauté until tender. Remove pot from heat and remove meat and onion from pot; pour off oil.

Return meat and onion to pot and add bell pepper. Pour prepared cola mixture over meat; season with salt and pepper as desired. Cover pot with lid.

Rearrange about ⅓ hot coals to make cooking ring underneath Dutch oven; place remaining hot coals on lid. Cook about 1 hour or until meat is tender and sauce thickens. Rotate pot and lid several times during cooking and replenish coals on top and bottom as needed to maintain cooking temperature. Serve with sauce and cooked noodles.

> **Variation:** Add ¼ cup teriyaki sauce and 1 teaspoon garlic powder while browning round steak. Do not drain. Add ¼ cup chopped jalapeño peppers and 1 teaspoon red pepper flakes before cooking.

STUFFED PORTOBELLO BAKE

Ingredients

- Portobello mushroom caps
- Mayo
- Chopped onions
- Canned tiny shrimp, drained
- Fresh basil
- Parmesan cheese
- Panko bread crumbs
- Olive oil

Directions

Remove the mushroom's stem and gills. Grease a pie iron; set the mushroom cap inside. Spread cavity with a little mayo. Toss on onions, shrimp and basil. Top with a handful of cheese and bread crumbs. Add a drizzle of oil and close iron. Cook without turning until the bread crumbs are toasted.

BARBECUED BEEF BRISKET

Serve slices of hot brisket with remaining sauce in Dutch oven.

Ingredients

- 1 (3 lb.) beef brisket
- 2 to 3 onions
- ½ C. ketchup
- ½ C. tomato soup
- 1 T. lemon juice
- 1 T. brown sugar
- 1 T. vegetable oil
- 1 tsp. salt
- ½ tsp. pepper
- Hot sauce to taste, optional

Preparation

Trim off excess fat from brisket. Chop onions and set aside. In a small bowl, combine ketchup, soup, lemon juice and brown sugar; mix well and reserve for later use.

★★★★ DUTCH OVEN DETAILS ★★★★

Safe Storage

Remove leftovers from cast iron cookware for storage or food may pick up a metallic taste.

DUTCH OVEN & CAST IRON COOKING

On the Stove

Place Dutch oven on stovetop over medium heat and add oil. When hot, brown brisket on all sides. Push meat to one side in pot. Add onions and sauté until tender. Add 2 cups hot water, salt, pepper and hot sauce, if desired. Cover with lid, reduce heat to low and simmer for 1 hour.

Pour reserved ketchup mixture over brisket. Cover and simmer slowly for 1¼ hours more or until meat is tender. Stir occasionally and add more water if necessary. Let brisket stand at least 10 minutes before slicing across the grain.

Over the Fire (22+ hot coals)

Spread hot coals in a flat layer underneath Dutch oven and add oil. When hot, brown brisket on all sides. Push brisket to one side in pot. Add onions and sauté until tender. Add 2 cups hot water, salt, pepper and hot sauce, if desired. Cover pot with lid.

Rearrange about ½ hot coals to make cooking ring underneath Dutch oven; place remaining hot coals on lid. Simmer about 1 hour, stirring occasionally and rotating pot and lid several times during cooking. Adjust the number of coals on top and bottom as needed to maintain cooking temperature.

Pour reserved ketchup mixture over brisket. Cover and simmer slowly for 1¼ hours more or until meat is tender. Stir occasionally and add more water if necessary. Rotate pot and lid several times during cooking and replenish coals as needed for even heat. Let brisket stand at least 10 minutes before slicing across the grain.

Alternate Cooking Method

If preferred, transfer Dutch oven from stovetop to a 300°F oven for the last 1¼ hours of cooking time.

DUTCH OVEN STROGANOFF

Serve over cooked noodles, rice or mashed potatoes.

Ingredients

- 2 lb. boneless sirloin steak
- 1 C. flour
- ½ tsp. salt
- ¼ tsp. pepper
- 2 to 3 T. vegetable oil
- 1 onion, sliced
- 1 tsp. minced garlic
- 1 (14.5 oz.) can beef broth
- 1 T. Worcestershire sauce
- 2 bay leaves
- ¼ tsp. paprika
- 1 C. sliced mushrooms
- 2 (.87 oz.) pkgs. brown gravy mix
- Hot cooked egg noodles, rice or mashed potatoes

Preparation

Cut steak into ½" x 2" strips. In a small bowl, stir together flour, salt and pepper. Coat steak strips with flour mixture.

★ ★ ★ ★ DUTCH OVEN DETAILS ★ ★ ★ ★

Lifestyles of the Rich and Famous

Cooking with cast iron is not just a popular trend among home cooks. In fact, inspired by the native cooking techniques in his home country of Argentina, renowned chef Francis Mallmann cooks with wood fire and cast iron cookware in his restaurants.

On the Stove

Place Dutch oven on stovetop over medium heat and add oil. When hot, brown steak strips on both sides. Push meat to one side and add onion; sauté until golden. Add garlic and sauté briefly. Stir in broth, 1¼ cups water, Worcestershire sauce, bay leaves and paprika. Bring to a simmer. Cover with lid, reduce heat to low and simmer for 1 to 1½ hours or until meat is almost tender.

Uncover and stir in mushrooms and gravy mix; cook until thickened, stirring frequently. Remove bay leaves before serving.

Over the Fire or on the Grill (24+ hot coals)

Spread hot coals in a flat layer underneath Dutch oven and add oil. When hot, brown steak strips on both sides. Push meat to one side and add onion; sauté until golden. Add garlic and sauté briefly. Stir in broth, 1¼ cups water, Worcestershire sauce, bay leaves and paprika. Bring to a simmer. Cover pot with lid.

Rearrange about ⅓ hot coals to make cooking ring underneath Dutch oven; place remaining hot coals on lid. Simmer for 1 to 1½ hours or until meat is almost tender. Rotate pot and lid several times during cooking and replenish coals on top and bottom as needed to maintain cooking temperature.

Remove lid and stir in mushrooms and gravy mix. Cover and cook until thickened, stirring twice. Remove bay leaves before serving.

Alternate Cooking Method
If preferred, after covering Dutch oven, transfer it to a 325°F oven to cook. Then finish on stovetop.

TENDER BEEF POT ROAST

SERVES 8

Ingredients

- 3 carrots
- 3 potatoes or sweet potatoes
- ½ C. flour
- 1 tsp. black pepper
- 1 (4 to 6 lb.) chuck roast
- ⅓ C. vegetable oil
- ¾ C. ketchup
- 2 tsp. minced garlic
- 1 (10.5 oz.) can French onion soup
- 1 (14.5 oz.) can beef broth

Preparation

Peel the carrots and potatoes; cut them into 2" pieces. Mix the flour and pepper on a large plate and coat all sides of roast in the flour mixture.

On the Stove

Place Dutch oven on stovetop over medium heat. Heat the oil and add the roast. Cook 4 to 5 minutes on each side until nicely browned; push the roast to one side of pot. Add the ketchup, garlic, carrots and potatoes; stir and cook about 5 minutes. Move roast back to the center of pot and arrange some vegetables on each side. Add soup and broth; cover pot with lid. Let food simmer slowly for 2½ to 3 hours or until beef is very tender, checking periodically.

Over the Fire (About 23 hot coals)

Spread about 23 hot coals in a flat layer under the Dutch oven. Heat the oil and add the roast. Cook 4 to 5 minutes on each side until nicely browned; push the roast to one side of pot. Add the ketchup, garlic, carrots and potatoes; stir and cook about 5 minutes. Move roast back to the center of pot and arrange some vegetables on each side. Add soup and broth; cover pot with lid.

Rearrange 7 of the hot coals in a ring under the Dutch oven and place remaining coals on the lid. Let food simmer slowly for 2½ to 3 hours or until beef is very tender. Maintain a simmer by letting coals burn down before replacing them. Rotate pot and lid every 15 minutes and check periodically; adjust heat as needed to prevent overcooking.

> **Tip:** Turn any fresh seasonal vegetables into a favorite campfire dish when you cook them like this.

SWISS CRABMEAT BAKE

SERVES
6

Ingredients

- 1½ C. flour, divided
- 1 tsp. salt, divided
- 2 tsp. baking powder
- 1¼ C. shredded Swiss cheese, divided
- 2 T. plus ½ C. butter, divided
- ½ C. chopped green bell pepper
- ½ C. chopped onion
- 1 tsp. dry mustard
- 1½ C. milk, divided
- 1 (8 oz.) pkg. imitation crabmeat
- ½ C. chopped Roma tomatoes
- 2 tsp. Worcestershire sauce

Preparation

In a medium bowl, combine 1 cup flour, ½ teaspoon salt and baking powder. Stir in ¼ cup Swiss cheese. With a pastry blender or two knives, cut in 2 tablespoons butter until mixture is crumbly; reserve for later use.

On the Stove and in the Oven

Preheat oven to 400°F. Meanwhile, place skillet on stovetop over medium heat and melt remaining ½ cup butter. Add bell pepper and onion; sauté until tender. Gradually blend in remaining ½ cup flour, dry mustard, 1 cup milk and remaining 1 cup cheese. Reduce heat to low and cook until cheese melts, stirring constantly. Add crabmeat, tomatoes and Worcestershire sauce; cook and stir until mixture is hot. Spread evenly in skillet and remove from heat.

To reserved flour mixture, add remaining ½ cup milk and stir until dough forms. Drop dough by small spoonfuls over hot crab mixture, like a cobbler topping. Transfer skillet to center rack in oven and bake uncovered about 25 minutes or until topping is golden brown and no longer doughy. Let cool slightly before serving.

Over the Fire (About 24 hot coals)

Arrange about ½ hot coals in cooking ring underneath Dutch oven. Melt butter in pot. Add bell pepper and onion; sauté until tender. Blend in remaining ½ cup flour, dry mustard, 1 cup milk and remaining 1 cup cheese. Remove about 4 hot coals from cooking ring to reduce heat; cook mixture until cheese melts, stirring constantly. Add crabmeat, tomatoes and Worcestershire sauce; cook and stir until mixture is hot.

Prepare dough and drop over hot crab mixture as directed above. Cover pot and place remaining hot coals on lid. Cook for 20 to 30 minutes or until topping is golden brown and no longer doughy. Rotate pot and lid twice during cooking and adjust the number of coals on top and bottom as needed for even cooking. Let cool slightly before serving.

FISHERMAN'S TUNA MELTS

Ingredients

- Canned tuna, drained
- Pickle relish
- Mayo
- Softened butter
- Rye bread
- Havarti cheese
- Tomatoes
- Salt & pepper

Directions

Stir together tuna, relish and mayo for tuna salad. Butter bread; butter side goes in pie iron. Add tuna mixture, cheese, a tomato slice, salt and pepper. Add another buttered bread slice with the butter face up; close iron. Trim crusts and heat in hot coals.

BLACKENED CAJUN CATFISH

Serve promptly, pouring reserved melted butter over catfish.

Ingredients

- 1 tsp. black pepper
- 1 tsp. cayenne pepper
- 1 tsp. garlic powder
- 1 tsp. onion powder
- 1 tsp. paprika
- 1 tsp. dried parsley
- 1 tsp. salt
- ½ tsp. dried oregano
- ½ tsp. dried thyme
- ¾ C. butter, melted, divided
- 4 (4 oz.) catfish fillets, skinned

Preparation

In a small bowl, mix black pepper, cayenne pepper, garlic powder, onion powder, paprika, parsley, salt, oregano and thyme. Press catfish fillets into spice mixture until well coated on all sides.

On the Stove

Place skillet on stovetop over high heat. Pour about ¼ cup melted butter into skillet; set remaining ½ cup butter aside. When butter in skillet is smoking hot, add catfish and cook until spices are burned onto fillets and fish is opaque and flaky inside, about 3 minutes on each side. Do not breathe smoke from burning spices.

Over the Fire or on the Grill (30 hot coals)

Place skillet on a grate over high heat (hot coals or gas grill) or set directly on a propane burner. Pour about ¼ cup melted butter into skillet; set remaining ½ cup butter aside. When butter in skillet is smoking hot, add catfish and cook until spices are burned onto fillets and fish is opaque and flaky inside, about 3 minutes on each side. Adjust the number and placement of coals as needed to maintain heat. Do not breathe smoke from burning spices.

Cast iron is great for cooking all of your favorite seafood, including salmon!

SIDE DISHES

No meal is complete without attractive, colorful sides, and as the recipes in this chapter show, common veggies plus cast iron equals bliss. Transform your potatoes and onions and baked beans into mouthwatering complements, or even prep some appetizers for a summer party using your best skillet and grill. And you'll make any chilly campsite feel like the center of the world with the aroma of baked beans set to the music of a crackling campfire. These recipes will show you how!

LOADED PARTY POTATOES

Serve promptly alongside any main dish.
Garnish with sliced green onions, if desired.

Ingredients

- 1 (10.7 oz.) can cream of chicken soup
- 1 (10.7 oz.) can cream of mushroom soup
- 2 C. sour cream
- 1½ C. shredded cheddar cheese
- ¼ tsp. pepper
- 1 (30 oz.) bag frozen shredded or cubed hash browns, partially thawed
- ⅓ C. chopped green onions
- 2 C. crushed corn flakes cereal
- ¼ C. butter, melted
- Sliced green onions, optional

Preparation

In a large bowl, combine both cans of soup, sour cream, cheese and pepper; stir to blend. Add hash browns and chopped green onions; mix well. In place of frozen hash browns, peel 12 large potatoes; boil in lightly salted water for 30 minutes or until almost tender. Cool completely. Grate or dice into a large bowl and proceed as directed.

★★★★ DUTCH OVEN DETAILS ★★★★

Removing Odors

To remove onion, garlic or fish odors from cast iron cookware, wipe with a little vinegar and then reseason as necessary.

In the Oven

Preheat oven to 350°F. Lightly grease Dutch oven with nonstick cooking spray. Spoon prepared potato mixture into pot and spread evenly.

In a small bowl, stir together cereal and melted butter; sprinkle evenly over potato mixture. Place pot on center rack in oven and bake uncovered about 40 minutes or until hot and bubbly. Let stand 5 minutes before serving.

Over the Fire (About 24 hot coals)

Lightly grease Dutch oven with nonstick cooking spray. Spoon prepared potato mixture into pot and spread evenly.

In a small bowl, stir together cereal and melted butter; sprinkle evenly over potato mixture. Cover pot with lid.

Arrange about ½ hot coals in cooking ring underneath Dutch oven. Place remaining hot coals on lid. Cook for 25 to 30 minutes or until hot and bubbly. Rotate pot and lid twice during cooking and adjust the number of coals on top and bottom as needed for even cooking. Let stand 5 minutes before serving.

Alternate Cooking Method

Use a kitchen-style Dutch oven with lid and cook on a grate over medium heat (hot coals or gas heat). Allow extra cooking time.

CHEESY PUFFED POTATOES

Serve hot alongside meat or fish dishes.

Ingredients

> 4 lb. russet potatoes, peeled
> 2 C. shredded cheddar or Swiss cheese, divided
> 1 ¼ C. milk

> 5 T. butter, softened
> 1 tsp. seasoned salt
> 2 eggs, beaten

Preparation

Cut potatoes into cubes.

★★★★ SKILLET SECRETS ★★★★

A Kitchen Must-Have

Did you know that HowStuffWorks listed cast iron skillets and pans as number two on their list of Top 10 Must-have Cooking Tools? According to John Fuller and Caitlin Uttley, professionals like cast iron because of its nonstick surface and lack of chemical coatings. If you care for your cast iron and keep it properly seasoned, it will produce delicious meals for years and years to come.

http://recipes.howstuffworks.com/tools-and-techniques/5-must-have-cooking-tools.htm

On the Stove and in the Oven

Preheat oven to 350°F. Meanwhile, place potatoes in Dutch oven and cover with water. Set on stovetop over medium heat and bring to a boil; cook until tender, about 20 minutes. Drain water and mash potatoes.

Stir in 1¾ cups cheese, milk, butter and seasoned salt. Cook and stir over low heat until cheese and butter are melted. Fold in eggs. Cover Dutch oven and transfer to center rack in oven; bake for 25 to 30 minutes. Remove lid and sprinkle with remaining ¼ cup cheese. Bake uncovered until golden brown, 5 to 10 minutes.

Over the Fire or on the Grill (About 24 hot coals)

Spread most of the hot coals in a flat layer underneath Dutch oven. Add potatoes and cover with water. Cover pot with lid and cook until tender, 20 to 30 minutes. Drain water and mash potatoes. Stir in 1¾ cups cheese, milk, butter and seasoned salt until cheese and butter are melted. Fold in eggs. Cover with lid.

Rearrange about ⅓ hot coals to make cooking ring underneath Dutch oven. Place remaining hot coals on lid. Cook for 25 to 30 minutes. Rotate pot and lid twice during cooking. Toward end of cooking time, remove coals from lid to make second ring around outside of pot. Remove lid and sprinkle remaining ¼ cup cheese over potatoes. Cook until melted, 5 to 10 minutes.

VINTAGE SPOTLIGHT

Griswold Odorless Skillet, circa 1898. With cover in place, this skillet was placed over the open hole of a wood or coal kitchen range. The concept was that the smoke and odors from the heat source would draw the fumes from the cooking surface down into the firebox, thus removing smoke and odor.

EASY POTATOES AU GRATIN

Let cool about 10 minutes before serving family style with a large spoon.

Ingredients

- 3 lb. russet potatoes, peeled
- 1 ¼ C. shredded cheddar cheese
- 1 ¼ C. shredded Monterey Jack cheese
- ½ C. grated Parmesan cheese
- 2 tsp. cornstarch
- ¾ C. heavy cream
- ½ C. low-sodium chicken broth
- ½ tsp. garlic powder, optional
- Salt and pepper to taste

Preparation

With a sharp knife or mandolin, thinly slice potatoes (about ⅛" thickness) and place in a large bowl. In another large bowl, combine cheddar, Monterey Jack and Parmesan cheeses with cornstarch and toss until evenly coated.

In a large measuring cup, combine cream, broth and garlic powder, if desired; stir to blend and reserve for later use.

In the Oven

Preheat oven to 350°F. Lightly grease Dutch oven with nonstick cooking spray. Layer ½ sliced potatoes in pot. Sprinkle potatoes with 1½ cups cheese mixture and season lightly with salt and pepper. Layer remaining potatoes over cheese and sprinkle with salt and pepper. Pour reserved cream mixture evenly over potatoes and top with remaining cheese mixture.

Cover pot with lid and place on center rack in oven to bake about 1 hour. Remove lid and bake uncovered for 15 to 20 minutes more or until golden brown and tender.

Over the Fire (26+ hot coals)

Lightly grease Dutch oven with nonstick cooking spray. Layer ½ sliced potatoes in pot. Sprinkle potatoes with 1½ cups cheese mixture and season lightly with salt and pepper. Layer remaining potatoes over cheese and sprinkle with salt and pepper. Pour reserved cream mixture evenly over potatoes and top with remaining cheese mixture. Cover pot with lid.

Arrange about ⅓ hot coals in cooking ring underneath Dutch oven. Place remaining hot coals on lid. Cook for 1 hour 20 minutes or until golden brown and tender. Rotate pot and lid every 15 minutes during cooking and replenish coals on top and bottom as needed to maintain cooking temperature.

CHEESE & ONION PUFFS

Serve with red bell pepper relish.

Ingredients

- Puff pastry
- Onion slices
- Swiss cheese
- Cheddar cheese
- Salt & pepper

Directions

Generously grease a pie iron. Cut pastry a little bit smaller than the iron; stretch to fit inside. Add an onion slice, cheeses, salt and pepper. A second pastry piece goes on top; seal edges. Close iron and cook over warm coals, turning often (if dough oozes out, just trim it off). When it looks like a little golden pillow, it's done.

SIMPLE GREEN BEANS &
RED POTATOES

Serve warm.

Ingredients
- 6 bacon strips
- 3 lb. fresh green beans
- 12 small red potatoes
- 1 onion
- 2 ¼ C. chicken broth, divided
- 2 tsp. salt
- ½ tsp. pepper
- ½ tsp. garlic powder
- ¼ to ½ C. butter, sliced

Preparation
Cut bacon strips into small pieces. Rinse green beans and remove ends; cut in half. Scrub potatoes and slice onion; set aside.

★★★★ SKILLET SECRETS ★★★★

The Home Test

New York Times columnist Marian Burros decided to conduct a home test to find the perfect skillet. Using 8 different pans, including aluminum, copper, carbon steel, bare cast iron and enamel cast iron skillets, she cooked eggs, chicken, onions and potatoes with varying amounts of oil. In the end, the cast iron skillets (both bare and enamel) came out on top. Burros found that they cooked the food beautifully and were a breeze to clean.

http://www.nytimes.com/2006/06/07/dining/07pans.html?pagewanted=all&_r=0

On the Stove

Place Dutch oven on stovetop over medium heat and add bacon; cook and stir until crisp. Add green beans to pot, stirring to coat. Stir in 2 cups broth, salt, pepper and garlic powder. Cover with lid and reduce heat to medium-low; cook for 20 to 30 minutes or until green beans are partially cooked.

Add potatoes and onion to pot and stir in remaining ¼ cup broth as needed. Cover and simmer slowly until potatoes are tender, about 30 minutes, checking often to keep some liquid in pot. When potatoes are tender, reduce heat to low and stir in butter as desired. When melted, cover pot and remove from heat to stand for 15 minutes or until green beans are wilted.

Over the Fire (26+ hot coals)

Spread hot coals in flat layer underneath Dutch oven. Place bacon in pot and cook until crisp. Add green beans, stirring to coat. Stir in 2 cups broth, salt, pepper and garlic powder. When hot, cover with lid and remove pot from heat.

Rearrange about ½ hot coals to make cooking ring underneath Dutch oven; place remaining hot coals on lid. Cook for 20 to 30 minutes or until beans are partially cooked, rotating pot and lid twice.

Add potatoes and onion; stir in remaining ¼ cup broth as needed. Cover and simmer slowly until potatoes are tender, about 30 minutes. Rotate pot and lid two more times during cooking and check to keep some liquid in pot. Replenish coals on top and bottom as needed to maintain cooking temperature. When potatoes are tender, remove Dutch oven from heat and stir in butter as desired. Cover and let stand for 15 minutes or until green beans are wilted.

GARLIC POTATO WEDGES

Ingredients
- 4 large russet potatoes
- ½ C. butter
- 3 T. grated Parmesan cheese
- ½ tsp. garlic powder
- 1 tsp. seasoned salt
- Dried parsley flakes

Preparation
Wash the potatoes and cut each into 8 wedges. In a small bowl, mix cheese, garlic powder and seasoned salt.

On the Stove and in the Oven

Preheat the oven to 350°F. Meanwhile, place Dutch oven on stovetop over low heat and melt the butter. Remove the pot from heat and coat potato wedges in butter; arrange them in a single layer in the pot. Sprinkle cheese mixture over the potatoes. Top with some parsley flakes.

Transfer Dutch oven to center rack in oven to cook uncovered for about 30 minutes or until potatoes are fork-tender.

Over the Fire (About 25 hot coals)

Set Dutch oven over a few hot coals and melt the butter. Remove the pot from heat and coat potato wedges in butter; arrange them in a single layer in the pot. Sprinkle cheese mixture over the potatoes. Top with some parsley flakes and cover pot with lid.

Set the Dutch oven on a ring of 9 hot coals and place about 16 coals on the lid. Cook about 30 minutes or until potatoes are fork-tender. Rotate pot and lid twice during cooking time and replenish coals on top as needed for even cooking.

CHEESY BAKED CORN

Ingredients

- 1 (15.2 oz.) can cream-style corn
- 1 (15.2 oz.) can whole kernel corn, drained
- ½ C. cornmeal
- 1 tsp. garlic salt
- ½ C. grated Parmesan cheese
- 1 ½ C. shredded cheddar cheese
- 1 tsp. baking powder
- ¼ to ½ C. vegetable oil
- 2 eggs, lightly beaten
- ½ tsp. onion powder, optional

Preparation

In a large bowl, combine cream-style corn, whole kernel corn, cornmeal, garlic salt, Parmesan cheese, cheddar cheese, baking powder and oil; mix well. Add eggs and stir to blend. Stir in onion powder, if desired.

★★★★ SKILLET SECRETS ★★★★

Professional References

Chef and cookbook author Sara Moulton is a huge fan of cast iron, and here's why:

"There is a reason that the cast-iron skillet, a favorite pan going all the way back to colonial times, is still popular. Even though it takes time to heat up, once hot, it retains the heat evenly for quite a while. Moreover, if you take good care of it and keep it well seasoned, it will behave like a nonstick pan. The more you use it the more nonstick it will become."

In the Oven

Preheat oven to 350°F. Grease bottom and sides of Dutch oven with nonstick cooking spray. Pour prepared corn mixture into pot and place on center rack in oven. Bake uncovered for 40 to 45 minutes or until lightly browned and heated through.

Over the Fire (22+ hot coals)

Grease bottom and sides of Dutch oven with nonstick cooking spray. Pour prepared corn mixture into pot and cover with lid.

Arrange about ⅓ hot coals in cooking ring underneath Dutch oven. Place remaining hot coals on lid. Cook for 35 to 45 minutes, rotating pot and lid several times during cooking and replenishing coals on top and bottom as needed to maintain temperature.

Variation
Add one 4-ounce can chopped green chilies for a little kick.

VINTAGE SPOTLIGHT

Spinning Broiler, circa late 1700s to mid-1800s. This is the larger of the two known sizes of this broiler type, and is an example of a very delicate casting. For use, coals from the fireplace were raked onto the hearth, where the spinning broiler was placed. The spokes of the wheel are concave to direct the juices from the meat being cooked into the reservoir in the center so they can be saved or used for basting.

VEGETABLE &
STUFFING BAKE

Serve family style with a large spoon while hot.

Ingredients

- 32 oz. assorted frozen vegetables, any combination, thawed (such as cauliflower, corn, broccoli, carrots, green beans or snow peas)
- 1 (6 oz.) pkg. cornbread stuffing mix, divided
- 1 T. vegetable oil
- ¾ C. chopped onion
- 1 tsp. minced garlic
- 1 (10.7 oz.) can cream of celery soup
- 1 C. Cheez Whiz
- 2 T. butter, melted, optional

Preparation

In a large bowl, combine vegetables and 1 cup dry stuffing mix; toss to combine and reserve for later use.

★★★★ SKILLET SECRETS ★★★★

Double Trouble

In general, if you use a Dutch oven or skillet larger or smaller than the size listed in a recipe, adjust the cooking time accordingly, allowing extra time for thicker mixtures or batters.

On the Stove and in the Oven

Preheat oven to 350°F. Meanwhile, place Dutch oven on stovetop over medium heat and add oil. When hot, sauté onion until tender. Add garlic and sauté briefly. Stir in soup and Cheez Whiz until blended; cook until heated through, stirring frequently.

Remove pot from heat and add reserved stuffing mixture; stir well to combine. Spread mixture in pot and sprinkle remaining dry stuffing mix over top. Drizzle with melted butter, if desired. Transfer pot to center rack in oven and bake uncovered for 30 to 35 minutes or until vegetables are tender and mixture is bubbly. Let stand several minutes before serving.

Over the Fire (About 22 hot coals)

Spread most hot coals in flat layer underneath Dutch oven. Pour oil into pot. When hot, sauté onion until tender. Add garlic and sauté briefly. Stir in soup and Cheez Whiz until blended; cook just until heated through, stirring frequently.

Remove pot from heat and add reserved stuffing mixture; stir well to combine. Spread mixture in pot and sprinkle remaining dry stuffing mix over top. Drizzle with melted butter, if desired. Cover with lid.

Arrange about ⅓ hot coals in cooking ring underneath Dutch oven. Place remaining hot coals on lid. Cook for 25 to 35 minutes or until vegetables are tender and mixture is bubbly. Rotate pot and lid twice during cooking and adjust the number of coals on top and bottom as needed for even cooking. Let stand several minutes before serving.

Alternate Cooking Method
Use a kitchen-style Dutch oven with a lid and cook on a grate over medium heat (hot coals or gas grill). Allow extra cooking time.

QUICK SPANISH RICE

Serve alongside meat, poultry or Mexican dishes.

Ingredients

- 1 green bell pepper, cored, seeded
- 1 red bell pepper, cored, seeded
- 2 celery ribs
- 2 onions
- 3 T. vegetable oil
- 2 C. uncooked white rice
- 2 tsp. cumin seeds, crushed
- 1 tsp. salt
- ½ tsp. pepper
- ¼ tsp. garlic powder
- 6 C. chicken broth (or water)
- 1 (8 oz.) can tomato sauce

Preparation

Finely chop bell peppers, celery and onions.

On the Stove

Place Dutch oven on stovetop over medium-high heat and add oil. When hot, add bell peppers, celery, onions, rice, cumin, salt, pepper and garlic powder. Sauté until rice is translucent and just beginning to brown, stirring frequently.

Stir in broth and tomato sauce until well combined. Bring mixture to a full boil. Reduce heat to medium-low, cover with lid and simmer slowly for 25 minutes or until rice is tender and liquid has been absorbed.

Over the Fire (About 26 hot coals)

Spread hot coals in flat layer underneath Dutch oven. Heat oil and add bell peppers, celery, onion, rice, cumin, salt, pepper and garlic powder. Sauté until rice is translucent and just beginning to brown, stirring frequently.

Stir in broth and tomato sauce until well combined. Bring mixture to a full boil and cover pot. Rearrange ½ hot coals to make cooking ring underneath Dutch oven. Transfer remaining hot coals to lid. Simmer slowly for 20 to 25 minutes or until rice is tender and liquid has been absorbed. Rotate pot and lid twice during cooking and adjust the number of coals on top and bottom as needed for even cooking.

> **Alternate Cooking Method:** Use a kitchen-style Dutch oven with lid and cook on a grate over medium heat (hot coals or gas grill). Stir frequently and adjust cooking time as needed.

INSIDE-OUT
JALAPEÑO POPPERS

Ingredients

- Corn flakes cereal
- Salt, pepper, garlic powder & cumin
- Whole grain bread
- Softened cream cheese
- Cheddar cheese
- Roasted red bell peppers, drained
- Jalapeño peppers

Tip: Wash hands after handling jalapeños.

Directions

Grease a pie iron. Crush cereal; stir in seasonings. Coat a bread slice with cooking spray; dip into crumbs. Set coated side face down in iron. Spread with a nice thick layer of cream cheese. Add cheddar and roasted bells. Slice jalapeños, remove seeds and add to iron. Spread cream cheese on a second bread slice; coat and dip the other side. Set bread on peppers, crumb side up. Close iron and trim; toast both sides.

GLAZED AUTUMN
VEGETABLES

Serve promptly, spooning extra glaze over vegetables.

Ingredients
- 3 parsnips
- 5 large carrots
- 1 butternut squash
- 2 sweet potatoes
- ½ C. butter

- ¾ C. brown sugar
- ¼ C. maple syrup
- 2 tsp. ground cinnamon
- 1 ½ tsp. ground nutmeg
- Salt and pepper to taste

Preparation
Peel parsnips, carrots, squash and sweet potatoes. Cut all vegetables into 1" chunks.

★★★★ SKILLET SECRETS ★★★★

Fashionable Cookware

Because of his reputation as a leading interior designer, you might not put Paul Fortune and cooking together. However, when asked about his favorite item by New York Times columnist David Colman, instead of selecting a favorite fabric or piece of furniture, Fortune raved about his cast iron skillet, which enables him to cook anything anywhere, from the stove to the grill to the fireplace.

http://www.nytimes.com/2012/09/16/fashion/designers-favorite-object-a-cast-iron-skillet-possessed.html

On the Stove and in the Oven

Preheat oven to 325°F. Meanwhile, place Dutch oven on stovetop over medium heat and melt butter. Stir in brown sugar, syrup, cinnamon and nutmeg until well blended. Add vegetables and toss to coat. Season with salt and pepper as desired.

Cover Dutch oven and place on center rack in oven to cook about 35 minutes. Remove lid, stir once and bake uncovered for 15 to 20 minutes more or until vegetables are tender and glazed.

Over the Fire (About 20 hot coals)

Arrange about ½ hot coals in cooking ring underneath Dutch oven. Melt butter in pot. Stir in brown sugar, syrup, cinnamon and nutmeg until well blended. Add vegetables and toss to coat. Season with salt and pepper as desired.

Cover pot and place remaining hot coals on lid. Cook for 30 to 35 minutes, rotating pot and lid twice during cooking. Adjust the number of coals on top and bottom as needed for even cooking.

Remove lid and stir once. Cook uncovered about 20 minutes more or until vegetables are tender and glazed, rotating pot and stirring again during cooking.

> ### Variation
> Recipe may be cut in half and cooked in a 10" skillet with lid as directed.

SPICY BAKED BEANS

Serve warm with sandwiches or grilled meats.

Ingredients

- 1 onion
- 1 green or yellow bell pepper, cored, seeded
- 1 (28 oz.) can plain pork and beans
- 1 T. chili powder
- 3 T. Worcestershire sauce
- 2 T. apple cider vinegar
- ½ C. brown sugar
- ½ C. ketchup
- 1 tsp. garlic powder
- Salt to taste
- Dash of cayenne pepper, optional

Preparation

Dice onion and bell pepper. Drain pork and beans.

In the Oven

Preheat oven to 350°F. Place onion and bell pepper in Dutch oven. Add beans, chili powder, Worcestershire sauce, vinegar, brown sugar, ketchup and garlic powder; stir until blended. Season with salt and cayenne pepper, if desired.

Cover with lid and place on center rack in oven. Bake for 1 hour, uncovering pot during the last 20 to 30 minutes to thicken sauce.

Alternate Cooking Method

Use a kitchen-style Dutch oven with lid and cook on a grate over medium heat (hot coals or gas grill). Stir often and adjust cooking time as needed.

10" with lid

Over the Fire (21+ hot coals)

Place onion and bell pepper in Dutch oven. Add beans, chili powder, Worcestershire sauce, vinegar, brown sugar, ketchup and garlic powder; stir until blended. Season with salt and cayenne pepper, if desired. Cover pot with lid.

Arrange about ⅓ hot coals in cooking ring underneath Dutch oven. Place remaining hot coals on lid. Cook for 1 hour, rotating pot and lid several times during cooking and replenishing hot coals on top and bottom as needed to maintain cooking temperature. During the last 20 minutes of cooking, carefully remove lid. Transfer several hot coals from lid to cooking ring underneath pot to maintain heat and promote thickening. Stir as needed.

ROASTED HERBED
VEGETABLES

Ingredients
- ¼ C. olive oil
- ¾ tsp. garlic salt
- ¾ tsp. dried oregano
- ½ tsp. dried thyme
- ¼ tsp. pepper
- ½ tsp. sugar
- 2 (12 oz.) pkgs. frozen vegetables (such as broccoli, cauliflower and carrots), partially thawed

Preparation
In a small bowl, combine oil, garlic salt, oregano, thyme, pepper and sugar; stir to blend.

In the Oven

Preheat oven to 425°F. Place vegetables in Dutch oven. Drizzle with oil mixture and toss to coat evenly. Spread vegetables in single layer in pot and place on center rack in oven. Roast uncovered for 20 to 25 minutes or until tender, stirring occasionally.

Over the Fire (About 36 hot coals)

Place vegetables in Dutch oven. Drizzle with oil mixture and toss to coat evenly. Spread vegetables in a single layer in pot and cover pot.

Arrange ⅓ to ½ hot coals in cooking ring underneath Dutch oven. Place remaining hot coals on lid. Cook for 15 to 25 minutes, stirring occasionally. Rotate pot and lid at least once during cooking and adjust the number of coals on top and bottom as needed for even cooking.

Try it on the grill!

ZUCCHINI-TOMATO BAKE

SERVES 8

Ingredients

- 1 onion
- 2 Roma tomatoes
- 3 zucchini
- 2 eggs
- ½ C. half-and-half
- ½ C. shredded cheddar cheese
- 1 T. olive oil
- 1½ tsp. minced garlic
- 1 tsp. ground thyme
- 1 tsp. salt
- 2 T. flour
- ¼ C. grated Parmesan & Romano cheese blend

Preparation

Chop onion and tomatoes. Slice each zucchini into ½-thick rounds; cut rounds in half.

In a small bowl, whisk together eggs and half-and-half. Stir in cheddar cheese and set aside. Then cook as directed on next page.

VINTAGE SPOTLIGHT

Victorian Gem Pan, circa 1850.

On the Stove and in the Oven

Preheat oven to 350°F. Meanwhile, place Dutch oven on stovetop over medium-high heat. Add oil; when hot, sauté onion and tomatoes until onion is tender. Add garlic and cook briefly. Stir in zucchini, thyme, salt and flour; cook until zucchini is tender.

Spread vegetable mixture in pot. Pour set-aside egg mixture over vegetables and sprinkle with Parmesan and Romano cheese blend. Bake uncovered for 30 to 35 minutes or until puffed and lightly browned on top. Serve promptly.

Over the Fire (About 22 hot coals)

Spread most hot coals in flat layer underneath Dutch oven. Heat oil in pot and add onion and tomatoes; sauté until onion is tender. Add garlic and cook briefly. Stir in zucchini, thyme, salt and flour and cook until zucchini is tender.

Spread vegetable mixture in pot. Pour set-aside egg mixture over vegetables and sprinkle with Parmesan and Romano cheese blend. Cover pot with lid.

Arrange about ⅓ hot coals in cooking ring underneath Dutch oven; place remaining hot coals on lid. Cook for 25 to 35 minutes or until puffed and lightly browned on top. Rotate pot and lid twice during cooking and adjust the number of coals on top and bottom for even cooking. Serve promptly.

DESSERTS

Sometimes you need something sweet. Who doesn't? And then there are those times when it just feels good to skip dinner and go straight to dessert. Not all the time, but now and then! With basic fruit ingredients like bananas, berries, pineapples or apples, plus a little dough and some sugar and other staples from the baking aisle, you'll turn your cast iron cooking area into a Parisian *boulangerie* in no time! Sweet, flaky pastries kissed brown by the hot iron turn any day into a special day. Why wait?

JUMBO CHIPPER COOKIE

Serve wedges alone or with ice cream.

Ingredients

- 2 ¼ C. flour
- 1 tsp. baking soda
- ½ tsp. salt
- ½ C. vegetable shortening
- ½ C. butter, softened
- ¾ C. sugar
- ¾ C. brown sugar
- 2 tsp. vanilla extract
- 2 eggs
- 1 C. semi-sweet chocolate chips
- 1 C. butterscotch chips
- Ice cream, optional

Preparation

In a medium bowl, whisk together flour, baking soda and salt. In a large mixing bowl, beat shortening and butter until creamy. Beat in sugar, brown sugar and vanilla. Add eggs and beat well. Gradually beat in dry ingredients until blended. Stir in chocolate and butterscotch chips.

In the Oven

Preheat oven to 350°F. Lightly grease skillet with nonstick cooking spray. Press prepared cookie dough evenly in bottom of skillet, flattening lightly. Bake about 30 minutes or until edges pull away from side of pan and top is golden brown. Remove from oven to a cooling rack and let cool in skillet for 15 minutes before removing from skillet or cutting into wedges.

Over the Fire (About 26 hot coals)

Lightly grease Dutch oven with nonstick cooking spray. Press prepared cookie dough evenly in bottom of pot, flattening lightly. Cover pot with lid.

Arrange about ⅓ hot coals in cooking ring underneath Dutch oven. Place remaining hot coals on lid. Cook for 25 to 35 minutes or until edges pull away from side of pot and top is golden brown. Rotate pot and lid several times during cooking and adjust the number of coals on top and bottom as needed for even browning. Uncover and let cool in Dutch oven for 15 minutes before removing from pot or cutting into wedges.

> **Tip:** Similar cookie recipes may be used following these cooking methods.

S'MORES HAND PIES

PIE IRON RECIPE

Ingredients

> Graham cracker crumbs
> Sugar
> Refrigerated pie crust
> Melted butter
> Whipped cream cheese
> Mini marshmallows
> Chocolate chips

Directions

Mix cracker crumbs with a little sugar. Cut crust into pieces to fit pie iron; dip in butter, then in crumbs. Set in iron; add some cream cheese. Toss in some marshmallows and chocolate chips. Dip a second crust piece in butter and crumbs; place on top. Close it up and set in warm coals until golden.

ONE-PAN BROWNIES

Serve warm or at room temperature with ice cream.

Ingredients

- 3 oz. unsweetened baking chocolate
- ¾ C. butter
- ½ C. sugar
- 1 C. brown sugar
- 3 eggs, lightly beaten
- 1 tsp. vanilla extract
- ¾ C. flour
- Ice cream

Preparation

Leave chocolate pieces in wrappers and hit with a rolling pin several times to break chocolate into small chunks; set aside. Cut butter into pieces.

On the Stove and in the Oven

Preheat oven to 325°F. Place skillet on stovetop over low heat and add chocolate pieces and butter. Cook and stir until melted and well blended.

Remove skillet from heat and stir in sugar and brown sugar until mixed. Whisk in eggs and vanilla. Add flour and whisk gently until all flour is incorporated. Scrape around sides of skillet and spread batter evenly.

Place skillet on center rack in oven and bake uncovered about 45 minutes or until brownies test done with a toothpick. Cool in skillet at least 15 minutes before cutting brownies into wedges.

Over the Fire (18+ hot coals)

Arrange about ⅓ hot coals in cooking ring underneath Dutch oven. Place chocolate pieces and butter in pot. Cook and stir until melted and well blended.

Remove Dutch oven from heat; stir in sugar and brown sugar until mixed. Whisk in eggs and vanilla. Add flour and whisk gently until all flour is incorporated. Scrape around sides of pot and spread batter evenly. Cover with lid.

Return Dutch oven to cooking ring and place remaining hot coals on lid. Cook for 30 to 40 minutes or until brownies test done with a toothpick. Rotate pot and lid several times during cooking and replenish coals on top and bottom as needed to maintain cooking temperature. Let cool at least 15 minutes before cutting brownies into wedges.

EXTREME BROWNIE PIE

PIE IRON RECIPE

Ingredients

- Ready-to-eat cheesecake filling
- Your favorite cookies
- Puff pastry
- Baked brownies

Directions

Coat a pie iron generously with cooking spray. Cut pastry into pieces smaller than the iron; stretch to fit in the bottom and up the sides. Set a brownie in the center. Add a dollop of cheesecake filling and set a cookie on top. Cover with another stretched pastry piece, pushing edges together to seal. Close the iron and cook slowly over warm coals, giving it time to bake the pastry and heat the filling.

NUTTY HOT FUDGE CAKE

Ingredients

- 1 ¼ C. sugar, divided
- 5 T. unsweetened cocoa powder, divided
- ½ C. brown sugar
- 1 C. flour
- 2 tsp. baking powder
- ¼ tsp. salt
- ½ C. milk
- 1 tsp. vanilla extract
- 2 T. butter, melted
- ¾ C. chopped pecans
- Ice cream, optional

Preparation

In a small bowl, mix ½ cup sugar, 2 tablespoons cocoa powder and brown sugar; set topping aside. In a medium bowl, stir together flour, remaining ¾ cup sugar, baking powder, salt and remaining 3 tablespoons cocoa powder. Add milk and vanilla; stir until blended. Stir in melted butter and pecans.

In the Oven

Preheat oven to 350°F. Grease bottom of Dutch oven with nonstick cooking spray. Line pot with a circle of parchment paper, extending paper 2" up sides; spray paper. Spread batter in Dutch oven. Sprinkle set-aside topping over batter. Pour 1 cup boiling water over top of cake but do not stir.

Place Dutch oven on center rack in oven and bake uncovered for 30 to 35 minutes or until cake tests done with a toothpick.

Remove from oven and let stand 5 to 10 minutes. Carefully invert cake onto a lightly greased platter. Remove parchment paper and cool at least 15 minutes before cutting.

Over the Fire (About 22 hot coals)

Prepare Dutch oven with nonstick cooking spray and parchment paper as directed above. Spread batter in Dutch oven. Sprinkle set-aside topping over batter. Pour 1 cup boiling water over top of cake but do not stir. Cover Dutch oven.

Arrange about ⅓ hot coals in cooking ring underneath Dutch oven. Place remaining hot coals on lid. Cook for 25 to 35 minutes or until cake tests done with a toothpick. Rotate pot and lid twice during cooking and adjust the number of coals on top and bottom as needed for even cooking.

Remove Dutch oven from heat and let stand about 5 minutes. Carefully invert cake onto a lightly greased platter. Remove parchment paper and cool at least 15 minutes before cutting.

FLAKY WALNUT PASTRIES

Ingredients

- Phyllo dough
- Chopped walnuts
- Cinnamon
- Brown sugar
- Butter
- Honey

Directions

Grease a pie iron. Stack five or six layers of dough, coating each with cooking spray. Cut stack into pieces a little bigger than your iron. Set one of these little stacks in the iron. Pile on walnuts; add cinnamon, brown sugar and some butter. Drizzle on a good amount of honey. Add another dough stack, close iron and trim. Hold over warm coals to toast slowly. Serve with extra honey and garnish as you see fit.

EASY SPICED PEACH CAKE

Serve warm in bowls topped with ice cream, if desired.

Ingredients

- 2 (21 oz.) cans peach pie filling
- 1 (18.25 oz.) pkg. spice cake mix
- 1 (12 oz.) can lemon-lime soda or ginger ale (not diet)
- Vanilla ice cream, optional

Preparation

Lightly grease bottom of 12" Dutch oven with nonstick cooking spray. Spread both cans of pie filling evenly over bottom of pot. Sprinkle dry cake mix over fruit. Pour soda evenly over cake mix and swirl lightly with a fork several times to moisten and partially blend.

In the Oven

Preheat oven to 350°F. Set Dutch oven on middle rack in oven and bake uncovered for 30 minutes or until bubbly around edges and cake is lightly browned on top and tests done with a toothpick. Let cool slightly before serving with a large spoon.

Over the Fire (24+ hot coals)

Cover Dutch oven with lid. Arrange about ⅓ hot coals in cooking ring underneath Dutch oven. Place remaining hot coals on lid. Cook for 30 to 40 minutes or until bubbly around edges and cake is lightly browned on top and tests done with a toothpick. Rotate pot and lid twice during cooking and replenish coals on top and bottom as needed to maintain cooking temperature. To promote browning on top, add several coals near handle on lid toward end of cooking time. Let cool slightly before serving with a large spoon.

Variation
Soda may be replaced with ¾ cup melted butter.

FRESH CINNAMON
FRUIT SWIRLS

Ingredients

- Refrigerated cinnamon rolls
- Softened cream cheese
- Fresh fruit of your choice
- Brown sugar
- Frosting

Directions

Flatten a roll and press into the bottom and up the sides of a greased pie iron. Spread with a little cream cheese; add fruit (mix and match as your mood dictates) and brown sugar. Flatten a second roll and set on top; press edges together. Close and heat slowly over warm coals until cooked and golden brown. Finish it off with a bit of frosting. Garnish as you please.

HIKER'S CHERRY ALMOND CAKE

Serve wedges at room temperature or warmed slightly.

SERVES
8

Ingredients

- 1 (10 oz.) jar maraschino cherries
- ½ tsp. vanilla extract
- ½ tsp. almond extract
- 2 C. flour
- 1 tsp. baking powder
- ½ tsp. salt
- ½ C. butter, softened
- 1 C. sugar
- 2 eggs
- 4 oz. white chocolate, chopped
- ½ C. sliced almonds
- 1 C. powdered sugar
- Milk

Preparation

Drain cherries and reserve ½ cup juice in measuring cup (add water if short). Add vanilla and almond extracts to juice. Cut cherries in half; set aside.

In medium bowl, stir together flour, baking powder and salt. In a large mixing bowl, beat together butter and sugar until light and fluffy. Add eggs, one at a time, beating well after each addition. Add flour mixture and cherry juice alternately to creamed mixture in bowl, beating on low until well blended. Fold cherries into batter.

★★★★ DUTCH OVEN DETAILS ★★★★

Golden Brown

To increase browning on top during the last few minutes of baking, lift the Dutch oven off the bottom coals and transfer those coals to the lid.

In the Oven

Preheat oven to 350°F. Grease skillet with nonstick cooking spray. Pour batter into skillet and sprinkle chopped chocolate over top. With a knife, gently swirl batter just to cover chocolate. Sprinkle with almonds. Bake uncovered for 1 hour or until cake tests done with a toothpick. Cool in pan for 15 minutes before inverting cake onto a wire rack to cool completely.

   Meanwhile, in a small bowl, whisk together powdered sugar with enough milk to make a thin glaze. Drizzle glaze over cake before slicing into wedges.

Over the Fire (24+ hot coals)

Grease Dutch oven with nonstick cooking spray. Line pot with parchment paper, if desired. Pour batter into pot and sprinkle chopped chocolate over top. With a knife, gently swirl batter just to cover chocolate. Sprinkle with almonds and cover pot with lid.

   Arrange about ⅓ hot coals in cooking ring underneath Dutch oven. Place remaining hot coals on lid. Cook for 50 to 60 minutes or until cake tests done with a toothpick. Rotate pot and lid several times during cooking and replenish coals on top and bottom as needed to maintain cooking temperature. Cool in pan for 15 minutes before inverting cake onto a wire rack to cool completely.

   Meanwhile, in a small bowl, whisk together powdered sugar with enough milk to make a thin glaze. Drizzle glaze over cake before slicing into wedges.

BANANA UPSIDE-DOWN CAKE

Serve warm or at room temperature with whipped topping, if desired.

Ingredients

> 5 fully ripe bananas, divided
> ½ C. buttermilk
> 1 tsp. vanilla extract
> 1½ C. flour
> ¾ tsp. baking soda
> ½ tsp. baking powder
> ½ tsp. salt
> ⅓ C. butter, softened

> 1¼ C. sugar
> 2 eggs
> 1 C. brown sugar
> 6 T. butter, melted
> 1 C. powdered sugar
> Milk
> Whipped topping, optional

Preparation

Peel and mash two bananas; measure 1 cup mashed fruit into a medium bowl. Add buttermilk and vanilla; stir well. In another bowl, whisk together flour, baking soda, baking powder and salt.

In a large mixing bowl, beat together softened butter and sugar until fluffy. Add eggs and beat well. Add dry ingredients and buttermilk mixture alternately to creamed mixture in bowl, beating until just combined.

In the Oven

Preheat oven to 350°F. Lightly grease Dutch oven and line with a circle of parchment paper, extending paper 2" up sides. Sprinkle brown sugar evenly over bottom of pot. Drizzle with melted butter. Peel and slice remaining three bananas and arrange slices in a single layer over brown sugar mixture. Spread prepared batter over banana slices.

Place Dutch oven on center rack in oven and bake for 35 to 40 minutes or until cake pulls away from side of pot and tests done with a toothpick. Let cake cool in Dutch oven for 20 minutes before carefully inverting onto a platter. Peel off parchment paper promptly.

In a small bowl, whisk together powdered sugar with enough milk to make a thin glaze. Drizzle over cake.

10" with lid

Over the Fire (22+ hot coals)

Lightly grease Dutch oven and line with a circle of parchment paper, extending paper 2" up sides. Sprinkle brown sugar evenly over bottom of pot. Drizzle with melted butter. Peel and slice remaining three bananas and arrange slices in a single layer over brown sugar mixture. Spread prepared batter over banana slices. Cover Dutch oven with lid.

Arrange about ⅓ hot coals in cooking ring underneath Dutch oven. Place remaining hot coals on lid. Cook for 30 to 40 minutes or until cake is golden brown and tests done with a toothpick. Rotate pot and lid several times during cooking and replenish coals on top and bottom as needed to maintain cooking temperature. Let cake cool in Dutch oven for 20 minutes before carefully inverting onto a platter. Peel off parchment paper promptly.

In a small bowl, whisk together powdered sugar with enough milk to make a thin glaze. Drizzle over cake.

CARAMEL BANANA
POUND CAKE

PIE IRON RECIPE

Serve with caramel sauce.

Ingredients

> Bananas
> Caramel-filled candy bars
> Pound cake
> Butter

Directions

Slice bananas and chop candy bars. Slice the cake to fit in your pie iron (lengthwise slices might fit best); butter one side of cake and lay butter side in iron. Layer banana slices and chopped candy bars on cake; cover with another cake slice, butter side up. Close iron and hold in warm coals; make sure you give it time for the candy bars to get gooey. Garnish any way you wish.

PINEAPPLE
UPSIDE-DOWN CAKE

Ingredients

- 1 (20 oz.) can pineapple rings
- 1 (20 oz.) can crushed pineapple
- 1 (18.25 oz.) pkg. yellow cake mix
- Eggs and oil as directed on cake mix package
- ¼ C. butter
- 1½ C. brown sugar
- 1 tsp. ground cinnamon
- ¼ C. sweetened flaked coconut, optional
- 10 maraschino cherries, drained
- Whipped topping

Preparation

Drain pineapple rings and crushed pineapple, reserving enough juice in a measuring cup to use in place of water listed on cake mix package (add water if short; discard any extra juice). In a large mixing bowl, combine cake mix, eggs, oil and pineapple juice; mix according to package instructions.

On the Stove and in the Oven

Preheat oven to 350°F. Meanwhile, place skillet on stovetop over medium heat and melt butter. Reduce heat and sprinkle brown sugar and cinnamon over butter, stirring to blend. Remove skillet from heat. Arrange pineapple rings over brown sugar mixture. Spread crushed pineapple over rings, pressing down lightly with a spoon. Press coconut on top, if desired. Set a cherry in each pineapple ring. Pour prepared cake batter over pineapple layer.

Transfer skillet to center rack in oven and bake uncovered for 30 to 35 minutes or until cake is lightly browned and tests done with a toothpick. Let cool in skillet for 5 to 10 minutes. Release edges of cake from skillet with a knife and carefully invert cake onto a platter. Let cool completely before slicing.

Over the Fire or on the Grill (26+ hot coals)

Arrange about ⅓ of the hot coals in a cooking ring underneath Dutch oven. Melt butter in pot and stir in brown sugar and cinnamon until blended. Remove pot from heat and arrange pineapple rings over brown sugar mixture. Spread crushed pineapple over rings, pressing down lightly with a spoon. Press coconut on top, if desired. Set a cherry in each pineapple ring. Pour prepared cake batter over pineapple layer. Cover pot with lid.

Return Dutch oven to cooking ring and place remaining hot coals on lid. Cook for 25 to 35 minutes or until cake is lightly browned and tests done with a toothpick. Rotate pot and lid several times during cooking and replenish coals on top and bottom as needed to maintain cooking temperature.

Remove from heat, uncover and let cake cool in Dutch oven for 5 to 10 minutes. Release edges of cake from pot with a knife and carefully invert cake onto a platter. Let cool completely before slicing.

PIE IRON
UPSIDE-DOWN CAKE

PIE IRON RECIPE

Ingredients
› Shortcakes
› Crushed pineapple, drained
› Brown sugar
› Butter
› Chopped pecans
› Maraschino cherries

Directions

Coat your pie iron with cooking spray. Set a shortcake in the iron, "well" side up. Fill the well with pineapple and brown sugar. Then add a little butter, some pecans and a cherry. Toast over warm coals until the cake starts to darken up a bit and the butter has melted, checking often. Garnish as desired.

BEST BERRY CRUMBLE

Serve warm or at room temperature in bowls,
topped with ice cream or whipped cream, if desired.

Ingredients

- 3 C. quick-cooking rolled oats
- ½ C. plus 2 T. whole wheat flour, divided
- 1 C. chopped pecans
- 1 C. brown sugar
- 1½ tsp. ground cinnamon
- 1 C. butter, cut into pieces
- 6 C. frozen berries (blueberries, raspberries, strawberries or any combination)
- ¼ C. sugar
- Ice cream or sweetened whipped cream, optional

Preparation

In a large bowl, stir together oats, ½ cup flour, pecans, brown sugar and cinnamon. With a pastry blender or two knives, cut in butter until mixture is crumbly.

In the Oven

Preheat oven to 400°F. Lightly grease skillet with nonstick cooking spray. Spread berries in pan. Sprinkle with sugar and remaining 2 tablespoons flour; toss gently to combine. Spread prepared oats mixture over top. Place on center rack in oven and bake about 30 minutes or until bubbly and golden brown. Let cool in skillet.

Over the Fire (About 30 hot coals)

Lightly grease Dutch oven with nonstick cooking spray. Line pot with parchment paper, if desired. Spread berries in pot. Sprinkle with sugar and remaining 2 tablespoons flour; toss gently to combine. Spread prepared oats mixture over top and cover pot with lid.

Arrange about ⅓ hot coals in cooking ring underneath Dutch oven. Place remaining hot coals on lid. Cook for 25 to 35 minutes or until bubbly and golden brown. Rotate pot and lid twice during cooking and adjust the number of coals on top and bottom as needed for even cooking. Remove lid and let cool in pot.

> **Variation:** In place of berries, try fresh or frozen chopped rhubarb, peaches or apples. Thaw and drain frozen fruits before using.

CAMPER'S DREAM PIES

PIE IRON RECIPE

Ingredients

> Refrigerated flaky biscuits
> Melted butter
> Cinnamon/sugar
> Raspberry jam
> Lemon pie filling

Directions

Coat your pie iron with cooking spray. Flatten a biscuit; coat with butter and sprinkle with cinnamon/sugar. Fit into pie iron; spread with jam and pie filling. Top with another coated biscuit; press edges together. Close iron and cook in warm coals until biscuits are done. Garnish any way you'd like, but it tastes great plain, too.

RHUBARB PIE DESSERT

Serve wedges warm or at room temperature.

Ingredients
- 2 eggs, beaten
- 1½ C. sugar
- Dash of salt
- 1¼ C. flour, divided
- 3 C. chopped rhubarb
- ⅓ C. powdered sugar
- ½ C. butter, cut into pieces

Preparation
In a large bowl, whisk together eggs, sugar, salt and ¼ cup flour until blended. Stir in rhubarb and reserve for later use. (If using frozen rhubarb, thaw and drain well before combining with other ingredients, patting dry if necessary.)

In a medium bowl, combine remaining 1 cup flour, powdered sugar and butter. With pastry blender or two knives, cut in butter until crust mixture is crumbly.

★★★★ SKILLET SECRETS ★★★★

Simple Sugar Solution

For easy cleanup, line cookware with parchment paper or heavy-duty aluminum foil when cooking anything with sugar.

In the Oven

Preheat oven to 350°F. Lightly grease skillet with nonstick cooking spray. Press prepared crust mixture into bottom of skillet and place in oven to bake for 12 minutes or until slightly browned.

Remove skillet from oven and let cool several minutes. Spread reserved rhubarb mixture evenly over warm crust. Return to oven and bake uncovered for 30 minutes more. Let cool at least 30 minutes before slicing and serving.

Over the Fire (About 24 hot coals)

Lightly grease Dutch oven with nonstick cooking spray. Press crust mixture into bottom of pot and cover with lid.

Arrange about ⅓ hot coals in cooking ring underneath Dutch oven. Place remaining hot coals on lid and bake crust for 10 to 15 minutes or until slightly browned.

Carefully remove lid. Spread prepared rhubarb mixture evenly over warm crust. Cover pot again and cook 25 to 35 minutes more. Rotate pot and lid twice during cooking and adjust the number of coals on top and bottom to reduce heat as needed to avoid overcooking. Let cool at least 30 minutes before slicing and serving.

Variation
In place of rhubarb, try fresh or canned peaches, pears or apples.

DUTCH OVEN CINNAMON-PECAN CAKE

Serve warm or at room temperature with a dollop of whipped topping or scoop of ice cream.

Ingredients

- 2 ¼ C. flour
- ½ tsp. salt
- 1 T. plus ½ tsp. ground cinnamon, divided
- 1 C. sugar, divided
- 1 C. brown sugar
- 1 tsp. baking powder
- 1 C. milk
- ½ C. vegetable oil
- 1 egg, beaten
- ½ C. chopped pecans
- Whipped topping or vanilla or cinnamon ice cream, optional

Preparation

In a medium bowl, stir together flour, salt, 1 tablespoon cinnamon, ¾ cup sugar, brown sugar and baking powder. In a large measuring cup, whisk together milk, oil and egg. Add milk mixture to dry ingredients and stir until batter is smooth.

In a small bowl, mix remaining ½ teaspoon cinnamon, remaining ¼ cup sugar and pecans; reserve topping for later use.

★ ★ ★ ★ DUTCH OVEN DETAILS ★ ★ ★ ★

Delightful Desserts

Because cast iron retains heat so well, foods finish baking after being removed from heat. Avoid over-cooking baked goods.

In the Oven

Preheat oven to 350°F. Line bottom of Dutch oven with a circle of parchment paper. Lightly grease paper and sides of pot with nonstick cooking spray. Spread batter evenly in pot. Sprinkle reserved topping mixture over top, swirling into batter lightly with a knife, if desired. Bake for 35 to 40 minutes or until cake tests done with a toothpick. Let cool slightly before slicing.

Over the Fire (About 22 hot coals)

Line bottom of Dutch oven with a circle of parchment paper. Lightly grease paper and sides of pot with nonstick cooking spray. Spread batter evenly in pot. Sprinkle reserved topping mixture over top, swirling into batter lightly with a knife, if desired. Cover Dutch oven with lid.

Arrange about ⅓ hot coals in cooking ring underneath Dutch oven. Place remaining hot coals on lid. Cook for 30 to 40 minutes or until cake tests done with a toothpick. Rotate pot and lid twice during cooking and adjust the number of coals on top and bottom as needed for even cooking.

APPLE CAKE DESSERT

Serve warm with ice cream.

Ingredients
- 2 eggs, lightly beaten
- 1 tsp. vanilla extract
- ½ C. melted butter
- 1 C. flour
- ½ C. sugar
- ½ C. brown sugar
- ¼ tsp. salt
- 1 tsp. ground cinnamon
- ½ tsp. ground nutmeg
- ¼ tsp. ground cloves
- 2 C. peeled, chopped apples
- ¼ C. chopped pecans
- 1 T. butter
- Vanilla ice cream

Preparation
In a large bowl, whisk together eggs, vanilla and melted butter until smooth; set aside. In a medium bowl, stir together flour, sugar, brown sugar, salt, cinnamon, nutmeg and cloves to blend. Add apples and pecans to flour mixture and toss until coated. Stir apple mixture into egg mixture until thoroughly combined.

In the Oven
Preheat oven to 350°F. Place skillet in oven to preheat about 5 minutes. Remove from oven and add 1 tablespoon butter. When melted, swirl skillet to coat bottom and sides. Pour batter into hot skillet and spread evenly.

Return pan to oven and bake uncovered for 40 minutes or until lightly browned and cake tests done with a toothpick. Let cake cool in skillet about 20 minutes before slicing into wedges.

Over the Fire or on the Grill (About 22 hot coals)
Arrange about ⅓ hot coals in cooking ring underneath Dutch oven. Add 1 tablespoon butter; when melted, brush over bottom and sides of pot. Pour batter into hot pot and spread evenly. Cover with lid.

Place remaining hot coals on lid. Bake for 20 to 30 minutes or until lightly browned and cake tests done with a toothpick. After about 15 minutes rotate pot and lid. Adjust coals on top and bottom as needed for even cooking. When done, remove lid and let cake cool in skillet about 20 minutes before slicing into wedges.

CARAMEL APPLE DELIGHT

PIE IRON RECIPE

Ingredients

- Angel food cake
- Apples
- Caramel dip
- Chopped peanuts
- Cinnamon/sugar

Directions

Set one cake slice in a generously greased pie iron. Cover with thinly sliced apples, caramel dip, peanuts and a generous dose of cinnamon/sugar. Add another cake slice. Close the iron; cook slowly in warm coals until the cake has browned evenly.

GRANNY'S APPLE PIE

Serve pie wedges with ice cream and caramel topping, if desired.

Ingredients

- 1 (14.1 oz.) pkg. refrigerated pie crust (2 ct.)
- 4 to 5 large apples (such as Granny Smith and/or Braeburn)
- ½ to ¾ C. sugar
- 2 T. brown sugar
- 1 tsp. ground cinnamon
- ⅛ tsp. ground nutmeg
- 2 T. flour
- 2 T. butter, cut into pieces
- Egg white, optional
- Coarse sugar, optional
- Ice cream, optional
- Caramel ice cream topping, optional

Preparation

Allow wrapped pie crusts to stand at room temperature for 15 minutes to soften. Peel and core apples; slice evenly. In a large bowl, mix sugar, brown sugar, cinnamon, nutmeg and flour; add apples and toss until coated.

In the Oven

Preheat oven to 350°F. Unroll one piecrust and press over bottom and up sides of skillet. Spread prepared apple mixture over crust. Dot with pieces of butter. Unroll remaining pie crust and place over apples, crimping crust edges together. If desired, whisk egg white until frothy and brush over piecrust; sprinkle with coarse sugar. Cut several slits in top crust to vent steam. Place skillet on center rack in oven (with baking sheet underneath) and bake uncovered about 1 hour or until golden brown and bubbly. Shield edges with aluminum foil if necessary to prevent excess browning. Cool for 30 minutes before slicing.

12"
with lid

Over the Fire (26+ hot coals)

Unroll one pie crust and press over bottom and up sides of a 9" deep metal pie plate, allowing excess crust to hang over rim. Spread prepared apple mixture over crust. Dot with pieces of butter. Unroll remaining pie crust and place over apples. Overlap crust edges and crimp to seal. If desired, whisk egg white until frothy and brush over pie crust; sprinkle with coarse sugar. Cut several slits in top crust to vent steam.

Prepare riser in Dutch oven (see page 95). Set pie plate on riser and cover pot with lid.

Arrange about ⅓ hot coals in cooking ring under Dutch oven. Place remaining hot coals on lid. Cook for 50 to 60 minutes or until golden brown and bubbly. Rotate pot and lid several times during cooking and replenish coals on top and bottom as needed to maintain cooking temperature. To promote browning on top, add several hot coals near handle on lid toward end of cooking time. Cool for 30 minutes before slicing.

Index